Why Be A Christian?

Darrell Pearson

Mark Oestreicher

David C. Cook Publishing Co.
Elgin, Illinois—Weston, Ontario

Custom Curriculum
Why Be a Christian?

Unless otherwise noted, Scripture quotations are from the Holy Bible, New International Version (NIV), © 1973, 1978, 1984 by International Bible Society. Used by permission of Zondervan Bible Publishers.

Published by David C. Cook Publishing Co.
850 North Grove Ave., Elgin, IL 60120
Cable address: DCCOOK
Series creator: John Duckworth
Series editor: Randy Southern
Editor: Lorraine Triggs
Option writers: Eric Potter, Nelson E. Copeland, Jr., and Ellen Larson
Designer: Bill Paetzold
Cover illustrator: Jim Carson
Inside illustrator: John Hayes
Printed in U.S.A.

ISBN: 0-7814-5011-X

CONTENTS

Sessions by Mark Oestreicher
Options by Eric Potter, Nelson E. Copeland, Jr., and Ellen Larson

About the Authors

Mark Oestreicher is the junior high pastor at Calvary Church in Santa Ana, California. He is also a free-lance writer and seminar leader.

Eric Potter is a free-lance writer living in Fredericksburg, Virginia. He is a former editor for the David C. Cook Publishing Co. He has written for several David C. Cook series including *Hot Topics Youth Electives* and *Pathfinder Electives*.

Nelson E. Copeland, Jr. is a nationally known speaker and the author of several youth resources including *Great Games for City Kids* (Youth Specialties) and *A New Agenda for Urban Youth* (Winston-Derek). He is president of the Christian Education Coalition for African-American Leadership (CECAAL), an organization dedicated to reinforcing educational and cultural excellence among urban teenagers. He also serves as youth pastor at the First Baptist Church in Morton, Pennsylvania.

Ellen Larson is an educator and writer with degrees in education and theology. She has served as minister of Christian education in several churches, teaching teens and children, as well as their teachers. Her experience also includes teaching in public schools. She is the author of several books for Christian education teachers, and frequently leads training seminars for volunteer teachers. Ellen and her husband live in San Diego and are the parents of two daughters.

You've Made the Right Choice!

Thanks for choosing **Custom Curriculum**! We think your choice says at least three things about you:

(1) You know your group pretty well, and want your program to fit that group like a glove;

(2) You like having options instead of being boxed in by some far-off curriculum editor;

(3) You have a small mole on your left forearm, exactly two inches above the elbow.

OK, so we were wrong about the mole. But if you like having choices that help you tailor meetings to fit your kids, **Custom Curriculum** *is* the best place to be.

Going through Customs

In this (and every) **Custom Curriculum** volume, you'll find
• five great sessions you can use anytime, in any order.
• reproducible student handouts, at least one per session.
• a truckload of options for adapting the sessions to your group (more about that in a minute).
• a helpful get-you-ready article by a youth expert.
• clip art for making posters, fliers, and other kinds of publicity to get kids to your meetings.

Each **Custom Curriculum** session has three to six steps. No matter how many steps a session has, it's designed to achieve these goals:

• *Getting together.* Using an icebreaker activity, you'll help kids be glad they came to the meeting.

• *Getting thirsty.* Why should kids care about your topic? Why should they care what the Bible has to say about it? You'll want to take a few minutes to earn their interest before you start pouring the "living water."

• *Getting the Word.* By exploring and discussing carefully selected passages, you'll find out what God has to say.

• *Getting the point.* Here's where you'll help kids make the leap from principles to nitty-gritty situations they are likely to face.

• *Getting personal.* What should each group member do as a result of this session? You'll help each person find a specific "next-step" response that works for him or her.

Each session is written to last 45 to 60 minutes. But what if you have less time—or more? No problem! **Custom Curriculum** is all about . . . options!

What Are My Options?

Every **Custom Curriculum** session gives you fourteen kinds of options:

• *Extra Action*—for groups that learn better when they're physically moving (instead of just reading, writing, and discussing).

• *Combined Junior High/High School*—to use when you're mixing age levels, and an activity or case study would be too "young" or "old" for part of the group.

• *Small Group*—for adapting activities that would be tough with groups of fewer than eight kids.

• *Large Group*—to alter steps for groups of more than twenty kids.

• *Urban*—for fitting sessions to urban facilities and multiethnic (especially African-American) concerns.

• *Heard It All Before*—for fresh approaches that get past the defenses of kids who are jaded by years in church.

• *Little Bible Background*—to use when most of your kids are strangers to the Bible, or haven't made a Christian commitment.

• *Mostly Guys*—to focus on guys' interests and to substitute activities they might be more enthused about.

• *Mostly Girls*—to address girls' concerns and to substitute activities they might prefer.

• *Extra Fun*—for longer, more "rowdy" youth meetings where the emphasis is on fun.

• *Short Meeting Time*—tips for condensing the session to 30 minutes or so.

• *Fellowship & Worship*—for building deeper relationships or enabling kids to praise God together.

• *Media*—to spice up meetings with video, music, or other popular media.

• *Sixth Grade*—appearing only in junior high/middle school volumes, this option helps you change steps that sixth graders might find hard to understand or relate to.

• *Extra Challenge*—appearing only in high school volumes, this option lets you crank up the voltage for kids who are ready for more Scripture or more demanding personal application.

Each kind of option is offered twice in each session. So in this book, you get *almost 150* ways to tweak the meetings to fit your group!

Customizing a Session

All right, you may be thinking. *With all of these options flying around, how do I put a session together? I don't have a lot of time, you know.*

We know! That's why we've made **Custom Curriculum** as easy to follow as possible. Let's take a look at how you might prepare an actual meeting. You can do that in four easy steps:

(1) *Read the basic session plan.* Start by choosing one or more of the goals listed at the beginning of the session. You have three to pick from: a goal that emphasizes *knowledge,* one that stresses *understanding,* and one that emphasizes *action.* Choose one or more, depending on what *you* want to accomplish. Then read the basic plan to see what will work for you and what might not.

(2) *Choose your options.* You don't *have* to use any options at all; the

basic session plan would work well for many groups, and you may want to stick with it if you have absolutely no time to consider options. But if you want a more perfect fit, check out your choices.

As you read the basic session plan, you'll see small symbols in the margin. Each symbol stands for a different kind of option. When you see a symbol, it means that kind of option is offered for that step. Turn to the page noted by the symbol and you'll see that option explained.

Let's say you have a small group, mostly guys who get bored if they don't keep moving. You'll want to keep an eye out for three kinds of options: Small Group, Mostly Guys, and Extra Action. As you read the basic session, you might spot symbols that tell you there are Small Group options for Step 1 and Step 3—maybe a different way to play a game so that you don't need big teams, and a way to cover several Bible passages when just a few kids are looking them up. Then you see symbols telling you that there are Mostly Guys options for Step 2 and Step 4—perhaps a substitute activity that doesn't require too much self-disclosure, and a case study guys will relate to. Finally you see symbols indicating Extra Action options for Step 2 and Step 3—maybe an active way to get kids' opinions instead of handing out a survey, and a way to act out some verses instead of just looking them up.

After reading the options, you might decide to use four of them. You base your choices on your personal tastes and the traits of your group that you think are most important right now. **Custom Curriculum** offers you more options than you'll need, so you can pick your current favorites and plug others into future meetings if you like.

(3) *Use the checklist.* Once you've picked your options, keep track of them with the simple checklist that appears at the end of each option section (just before the start of the next session plan). This little form gives you a place to write down the materials you'll need too—since they depend on the options you've chosen.

(4) *Get your stuff together.* Gather your materials; photocopy any Repro Resources (reproducible student sheets) you've decided to use. And . . . you're ready!

The Custom Curriculum Challenge

Your kids are fortunate to have you as their leader. You see them not as a bunch of generic teenagers, but as real, live, unique kids. You care whether you really connect with them. That's why you're willing to take a few extra minutes to tailor your meetings to fit.

It's a challenge to work with real, live kids, isn't it? We think you deserve a standing ovation for taking that challenge. And we pray that **Custom Curriculum** helps you shape sessions that shape lives for Jesus Christ and His kingdom.

—The Editors

Talking to Junior Highers about Why to Be a Christian

by Darrell Pearson

Sometimes I'm not sure why I'm a Christian. Sometimes it just seems like the thing to do. Maybe I'm a Christian because most of my friends are Christians. Or perhaps it's due to the way my parents brought me up. Or maybe it's because the Christian life is familiar and comfortable. My life is not always filled with the spiritual vitality that could land me a guest spot on the *700 Club* or turn my city upside down with excitement. Often I'm just acting the part, being a Christian because I've, well, *always* been a Christian (or so it seems).

Sounds like a junior high kid talking. Junior highers are really not much different from us, if we're honest about it. Many of them are Christians—or pretend to be Christians—because their friends are, because their parents have trained them well, or because it's the life they've always known. The "I'm-so-pumped-because-I've-just-found-the-Lord" mentality of the new Christian is generally left for high schoolers; junior highers who are new to the faith have a hard time articulating their discovery or really understanding the new joy. Sometimes, junior highers are not sure why they are Christians.

Junior highers, almost without exception, will come to grips with this problem in the eighth or ninth grade. Studies have shown that ninth grade is the time when students choose the Christian life or decide it's time to start sleeping in on Sundays. It's the first time that they've ever really considered the option of *not* accepting the faith. For once in their lives they are in the position of making the decision themselves. And *that* fact is very puzzling, frightening, and threatening to those of us who are trying desperately to pass on the faith to the next generation.

My own parents were scared to death of my rejection of the faith (though they didn't tell me at the time). My dating a non-Christian girl and my resultant drift away from the church led them to question my youth pastor about what they could do. His advice? Give him time. . . .

The Secret of Life in Twenty-Five Words or Less

I think most Christian adults have an extremely difficult time articulating what their faith means to them. Isn't that strange? We spend hours, days, months, years in study to grow as Christians; yet most of us (including us full-time youth directors) couldn't answer the simple question "Why are you a Christian?" in a few words. Why is this? You would think it would be the easiest thing in the world to do, but it isn't. Maybe the process is so ongoing and so lifelong that we just can't get an easy handle on it ourselves. So why are we so threatened by junior highers questioning their faith?

They're Too Much Like Us

I think most of us would agree that it's difficult for adults to believe and follow Christ. By the same token, it's equally difficult to watch students struggle with their faith. Helping and observing someone else struggle with the same difficulty you face is not easy.

I remember the first time my daughter Hilary was hurt by other kids calling her a name. It hurt to watch her struggle to understand why the kids did this, partly because it brought up so many memories buried in my own mind. (When you're the shortest kid in a school of three thousand, you get called a few names!) I didn't want her to go through these problems, but she had to. I could help as she dealt with the comments, but I couldn't keep her from experiencing life. When she gets older, she too will be in the ninth grade, and will start to wonder if it's worth being a Christian. It's still hard for me to follow Christ, and it will be hard to watch her as she chooses what to do. Strange paradox: I know that I struggle with following Jesus, but I have a hard time accepting that my child might do the same.

So, Why Are You . . . ?

Come up with *something!* Can you answer the great question? If not, you need to be able to. Not being able to give an account to students for the central motivation in your life is a pretty sad state.

When I was starting my youth ministry career I interned at a church in Iowa. One of the volunteers asked me one day, "How much do you love the Lord?" She expected an eloquent exposition I'm sure, but got a dumbfounded response that puzzled her. I spent years trying to answer that question. I still am. But I think now I could give a much clearer response about why I choose to follow Christ. With maturity, I've learned His provision for my life, my unworthiness, His grace. *Now* I think I could answer her question better. Junior high students are at the most critical age to make a decision about following Christ. Will they hear some wise words from us?

Be Like Me, For I Am Like . . . Christ!

That's what Paul said, even though it sounded a little haughty. He knew that even though it wasn't healthy for people to become overdependent upon a personality, to some extent a committed Christian is the best picture of Christ that others will see. What picture of Christ do your students see in you? If you are striving to be Christlike, your junior highers will never forget that image. I know. It's why I'm a follower today.

My college years involved the common search-and-destroy method of faith building: search for other answers, slowly let your faith die. It wasn't until I was halfway through college that I realized that all of the wonderful non-Christian friends I had associated with for two years had one desire for my life, which was for me to drink alcohol. The realization that this was their level of great concern for me prompted me to start looking for new friends. Where could they be found? Why, in the people who had always cared for me in the first place, the people from my Christian past I had grown up with. A look back at these people brought me back to the journey, because I knew they cared. Did you have a similar time in your life? A story of drifting and recovery? I'll bet in your return to the faith, there were people involved, maybe ones from your past.

That's the role you want to fill for your students. In the midst of their throwing pencils out the window, making cutting remarks about the Bible, belching at three in the morning on a retreat, they are somehow formulating a picture of the Christian faith for the future—and it's based on you, the nearest portrait of Christ they might ever see.

A Reason to Live

As students process the ideas and concepts in their lives that give direction to where they are going, they will most likely develop a growing awareness that their lives must revolve around some purpose. In the early years of middle school/junior high, those purposes are very simple: developing a self-image, growing a desire for material things, developing power, learning success in relationships, becoming independent. As kids move into high school, their ability to consider broader issues will lead them to discover that there are more important things in this world to build their lives around. They, just like us, will need a purpose for their lives. What will help them discover the greatness of following Christ is a close study of the leaders who, because they have chosen to follow Him, were willing to spend time with hard-to-love junior high students.

Darrell Pearson is co-founder of 10 to 20, an organization dedicated to presenting high-involvement events for teenagers. Formerly youth director at the First Presbyterian Church in Colorado Springs, Darrell spent most of his eleven years there directing the junior high program. He's co-authored Creative Programming Ideas for Junior High Ministry *(Youth Specialties), and written and presented the national-touring program* Next Exit. *He also speaks frequently to youth groups and leaders around the country. He lives with his wife and three daughters in Colorado Springs, Colorado.*

The images on these two pages are designed to help you promote this course within your church and community. Feel free to photocopy anything here and adapt it to fit your publicity needs. The stuff on this page could be used as a flier that you send or hand out to kids—or as a bulletin insert. The stuff on the next page could be used to add visual interest to newsletters, calendars, bulletin boards, or other promotions. Be creative and have fun!

Is This What It Means to Be a Christian?

What does it mean to be a Christian, anyway? Is it really worth it? What if it's not for real? We're starting a new course called *Why Be a Christian?* Come and find the answers you need.

Who:

When:

Where:

Questions? Call:

Why Be a Christian?

Why Be a Christian?

Check it out.

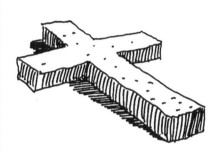

You won't believe your eyes!

Think about it.

Doubt Busters.

I Doubt It!

YOUR GOALS FOR THIS SESSION:

Choose one or more

☐ To help kids identify some of the spiritual doubts they might have.

☐ To help kids understand that having honest doubts is not sinful.

☐ To help kids choose one doubt to attack, using the "SCRAM" method.

☐ Other _____

_____

Your Bible Base:

John 20:24-30
Acts 17:10, 11

The "I Doubt It" Game

Divide your group into two teams. Explain that you're going to read a list of world records. Some are actual records and others are made up. Each team has to decide whether the record is real or fake. If the team thinks the record is fake, team members should shout out "I doubt it!" as loud as they can. If the team thinks the record is real, members should keep quiet.

Point to Team 1, read the first statement, and give team members a chance to make up their minds. Award one point for each correct response (or lack of one). Go back and forth between the two teams until you've gone through the list. Declare a winning team and have members cheer for themselves. Here is the list of records.

1. A man rode a 145-mile wheelie on a motorcycle. (Real.)

2. One man was struck by lightning seven different times. (Real.)

3. A woman kept a Hula Hoop going for 193 consecutive hours. (Fake.)

4. The largest Easter egg hunt involved over 72,000 eggs. (Real.)

5. The longest bicycle ever made held 47 riders. (Fake.)

6. The longest tunnel is 105 miles long. (Real.)

7. The biggest pumpkin ever grown was almost 6 feet high. (Fake.)

8. Two men played tennis for 8 days straight without sleeping. (Fake.)

9. Twenty-eight snow skiers did a back flip while holding hands. (Real.)

10. The biggest ice-cream sundae was 10 feet tall. (Real.)

11. One man received a 10,000 year prison sentence. (Real.)

12. A man ate 42 bananas in 3 minutes. (Fake.)

STEP
2

Dozens-O-Doubts

(Needed: Copies of Repro Resource 1, pencils)

Before passing out copies of "Dozens-O-Doubts" (Repro Resource 1) and pencils, ask group members to react to this comment: **When a person has doubts about his or her faith, he or she may not be a true Christian.**

Ask a few kids to explain their answers. You may want to point out that this may very well be true in some situations. In other cases, a person might be asking honest questions that deserve honest answers.

Hand out copies of Repro Resource 1 and instruct group members to put a check in the box that best describes their thoughts and feelings about each doubt.

After about five minutes, regroup and ask for a few responses to the following questions.

Which doubts on this list never bother you?

Which ones bug you a lot?

What are some other doubts kids have about God and Christianity that weren't on this list?

Then say: **Take a look at what you checked off for the last doubt on the sheet: "I doubt that it's OK to have doubts." Do you sometimes wonder if God will "zap" you if have doubts or questions about Him or the Bible?**

STEP
3

Doubting Thomas

(Needed: Bibles)

Choose one of your kids who's a good sport to roleplay a quick conversation with you. Ask this kid to tell you about the best vacation he or she ever went on, or some other memorable event. As he or she talks to you, interrupt with comments such as these: **Oh, really? Are**

you sure? or even a rather skeptical sounding **Hm-m-m.** Sound extremely doubtful of whatever the person says. When the kid has finished talking, it would be a good idea to assure him or her that you believed his or her story—honest!

Then ask: **How would you feel if people doubted *everything* you said?**

But what if a friend had a serious question about something you said, how would you prove it was true? (You could try to find some evidence or another person to back up what you're saying. You'd want to show that what you're saying is accurate and true.)

Explain that you're going to be looking at two instances in the Bible to see how the apostles and Jesus Himself reacted to people who had doubts about their message. Remind group members to keep in mind the last doubt on the "Dozens-O-Doubts" worksheet—"I doubt that it's OK to have doubts."

Have group members turn in their Bibles to Acts 17:10, 11. Fill in the details by explaining that Paul, Silas, and Timothy were traveling from city to city instructing people about their faith. Have a volunteer read aloud the two verses. Then ask: **What was going on in Berea? If these people were so noble, why did they check out Paul's message? Why didn't they just accept what Paul was saying?**

You might want to mention that Berea was a large, cosmopolitan city (today it's a ski resort!). People who lived there were open-minded and probably had heard all sorts of ideas—from the weird to the wacky to the wise. These people probably wanted to be sure Paul wasn't a religious kook.

Was it OK for them to do check out what Paul said? Give kids a chance to express their opinions. If necessary, point out that these individuals went to the right source, Scripture, to check out Paul's message.

Next, ask group members to turn in their Bibles to John 20:24-30. Have a volunteer read aloud this passage. Set the stage by explaining that Jesus had already died on the cross, had been buried, had risen from the dead, and had appeared to all the disciples—except Thomas.

Say: **Meet the original Doubting Thomas. Thomas wasn't a traitor like Judas Iscariot, but sometimes he gets a bad rap. How would you describe Thomas?**

Call on two or three kids who are familiar with this story to describe Thomas. For example, Thomas was a realist. He wasn't going to believe anything he hadn't seen. Thomas may have been timid or afraid, but with good reason. He and the other disciples had just witnessed Jesus' gruesome death, and word was out that the religious leaders wanted to kill the disciples too.

Look at the way Jesus handled Thomas's doubt. What does this tell you about Jesus? (Jesus accepts us—doubts and all.

He wants to help us stop doubting and believe.)

Explain: **Jesus didn't yell at Thomas and tell him it was wrong for him to doubt. In fact, Jesus did the opposite—He wanted to help Thomas work through his doubts and believe.**

Refer to Repro Resource 1 again. Point to the last doubt ("I doubt that it's OK to have doubts") and ask: **Based on what we've been talking about, would you change your answer to this last doubt?**

Pause for a minute to give kids a chance to reevaluate their responses, and then say: **Remember these two things: It's not un-Christian to have doubts, and Jesus can help us get the doubt out!**

SCRAM

(Needed: Copies of Repro Resource 2, chalkboard and chalk or newsprint and marker)

Ask group members what they would say to someone who is pesky (like a younger brother or sister) to get rid of him or her. If they don't come up with this themselves, suggest the command, "Scram!"

Have your group members shout, "Scram!" several times, teasing them with comments such as, **Oh, that's not loud, I can hardly hear you,** and **Is that really as loud as you can yell?**

Then pass out copies of "The SCRAM Doubt-Removal System" (Repro Resource 2). You'll need a chalkboard and chalk or newsprint and a marker for this exercise. Write the letters *S, C, R, A,* and *M* down the left side of the board.

Explain that the *S* stands for "Seek God's help." Instruct your group members to write this next to the S on their sheets while you write it on the board.

Say: **Before tackling any doubts, we have to pray—even if you have doubts about prayer. Just do it! Ask God to help you work through your doubts. He promises us He will!**

Next, explain what the *C* stands for: "Call it what it is." Have kids write this next to the *C* on their outlines while you write it on the board.

We need to be really honest with ourselves about our doubts. Sometimes it's easier to pretend we don't have doubts than to admit that we do. If you have doubts about God's forgiveness, tell God. Be specific. God can take it!

Then tell your group members that the *R* stands for "Read what the Bible says." Again, have group members write this on their outlines while you write it on the board.

The Bible is God's main way of communicating with us, so we need to read His Word. Maybe you could read one of the Gospels, like the Book of John, or a book like Ephesians.

Take a minute to review the first three steps in the method. Have group members turn their papers over. Then ask them what the *S*, *C*, and *R* stand for.

And the A stands for "Ask people you trust." This step helps out when those doubts refuse to budge. It's important to get the input of other people who love God. These people may have struggled with some of the same doubts you're struggling with, and you can learn from their experiences and advice. Or someone like a youth leader or pastor can help you understand what the Bible has to say.

Review the first four letters. Then tell your group members that the last letter, *M*, stands for "Make a decision and move on." Have your group members write this on their outlines as you write it on the board.

There comes a point when you need to make a decision about specific doubts. Either you've found enough help from the Bible and other sources that you can put a doubt behind you and move on—or you might need to keep applying the SCRAM Doubt-Removal System to get the doubt out.

It might take time for you to work through some doubts, but keep working at it. Some people lug around the same doubts all their lives only because they never do anything about them.

Review the whole process until you're confident your group members can remember the five points.

Pick a Doubt

(Needed: Different colored markers)

Set out several markers and ask kids to choose two different colors. Then have group members skim the "Dozens-O-Doubts" list from Repro Resource 1.

Explain: **Use one color and put a star next to your top three doubts. Next, use the second color, and write the word "SCRAM" in big, bold letters over the one doubt you want to confront.**

Quickly go over the SCRAM method one last time: Seek God's help; Call it what it is; Read what the Bible says; Ask people you trust; and Make a decision and move on.

Take care of the first step in the process by leading group members in prayer. Challenge kids to practice the SCRAM method on their chosen doubts.

Dozens-O-Doubts

	BIG TIME	SOME	A LITTLE	NOT!
1. I doubt God exists.				
2. I doubt Jesus Christ is really God's Son.				
3. I doubt God really cares about me.				
4. I doubt that Jesus never sinned.				
5. I doubt that heaven really will be all that great.				
6. I doubt that hell exists.				
7. I doubt a loving God would send people to hell.				
8. I doubt that God listens to everyone's prayers.				
9. I doubt God answers my prayers.				
10. I doubt the Bible doesn't have mistakes.				
11. I doubt that demons and angels exist.				
12. I doubt that miracles, like raising people from the dead, ever happened.				
13. I doubt that it's very important for me to read the Bible.				
14. I doubt God has good plans for my life.				
15. I doubt that God understands what my family is like.				
16. I doubt God can forgive some of the things I've done.				
17. I doubt that going to church is very important.				
18. I doubt God is with me all the time.				
19. I doubt that I'll ever be able to say no to some temptations.				
20. I doubt the story of Creation is accurate.				
21. I doubt Jesus will ever come back—at least not in my lifetime.				
22. I doubt God really cares about all the bad stuff going on in the world.				
23. I doubt that it will matter much if I wait a few more years to "get serious" about God.				
24. I doubt that it's OK to have doubts.				

THE SCRAM Doubt-Removal System **2**

S

C

R

A

M

Step 3

One way to increase our understanding of the Bible is to read it imaginatively—that is, to imagine how the people involved in the stories of Scripture might have felt in various situations. Help your group members do this by having them write skits based on the passages in this step. Have group members pair up for this activity. Instruct the pairs to make up conversations and reactions that might have taken place among the people involved in these Bible events. The skits should reveal the character of the people in the passage, their motivations, and how others might have reacted to what happened. Prod group members' creativity with questions like these: **What do you think the Bereans said about Paul's teaching? How might the people with Paul have reacted to the Bereans' skepticism? How would the disciples have responded to Thomas's doubts?** (For example, Peter might have said something like, "Are you calling me a liar?") Encourage the pairs to be humorous and accurate in their skits. Give them a few minutes to work; then have them perform their skits.

Step 4

Since the SCRAM principles involve reading what the Bible says and asking people you trust, give group members an opportunity to respond to doubts by staging a debate. Determine one of the main doubts held by your group. Then divide into two teams. One team should prepare to argue *against* the doubt; the other should prepare to argue *for* it. For example, one team could argue that God doesn't exist; the other could argue that He does. Give the teams five minutes to prepare their arguments. Then give each side one minute to present its view and thirty seconds to respond to its opponent's view. Afterward, point out that belief is grounded in faith but has support in reason, revelation, and fact.

Step 2

Depending on the maturity of your group members and their closeness, you may want to have all of them, rather than a few volunteers, share the results of their sheets. As a leader, you might want to get kids started by sharing your own doubts. It can be comforting for kids to know that they're not the only ones with doubts. Such honesty can also build unity and a sense of dependence on each other. For some of your group members, you may be one of the "trusted people" with whom they share their doubts privately. (See the "SCRAM" principles in Step 4.) Hearing you share your own doubts may inspire them to come to you with some of their more personal doubts.

Step 5

If you're group is small, you have the opportunity to apply two of the SCRAM principles ("read what the Bible says" and "ask people you trust") to your kids' most pressing doubts. Have each group member write his or her number-one doubt on a slip of paper. Collect the slips in a paper bag. Then pull out a slip and read the doubt. Ask volunteers to call out pertinent Bible passages and give their views as to why they believe, rather than doubt, this point. If possible, try to address the doubts on all of the slips.

Step 1

The opening quiz would be difficult for a large group to do as a contest, since large teams would have trouble reaching a consensus about the statements. So try this variation. Read one of the statements aloud. If group members think it's a real record, they should stand up. If they think it's fake, they should remain seated. After group members have responded to each statement, give the correct answer. (You may want to figure out a "gullibility percentage" or have group members keep their personal score and applaud those with the best records.) To add excitement to the activity, eliminate those who are wrong after each round. Afterward, discuss group members' basis for choosing whether or not to doubt something.

Step 3

Get more group members actively involved in the Bible study by breaking them into teams of four or five people. Have half of the teams look up the Acts passage and the other half look up the John passage. Instruct the teams to do profiles of the people in their passages, either of the "typical" Berean or of Thomas. Encourage them to think of the traits that these people exhibited. In creating the profiles, team members might write down a list of traits or they might use poster board and markers to make posters depicting the characters. Give the teams a few minutes to work. Then have each team share its list or poster and summarize its passage.

Step 2

Despite assurances that "it's OK to have doubts," kids who've been raised in the church may feel that adults, particularly church leaders, never have any doubts. After all, few kids have probably ever heard a pastor or speaker say, "I have a really hard time believing this principle." Address the feelings of these kids with the following questions. Ask: **Do you think your pastor ever has any doubts about the Bible or his faith? Why or why not? If he did have doubts, would you want him to share those doubts with the church? Why or why not? How do you think the church would respond if the pastor shared his doubts? How would you respond? How might a non-Christian visitor to the church respond?**

Step 4

Some of your kids may be struggling with what appears to them to be circular logic: God exists because the Bible says so and the Bible is true because it's God's Word. Point out that, ultimately, belief is a gift from God, a matter of faith—but it's not a blind leap. There are evidences for the trustworthiness of Scripture and, while they might not absolutely *prove* the Bible is true, they can be persuasive. Get group members thinking about the problems of proof and persuasiveness by having them play a game in which they must prove their identity. Ask a volunteer to state who he or she is. The rest of the group members should ask for proof of the person's claims. As the volunteer offers various proofs (ID card, library card, testimony of friends, swearing on a stack of Bibles, etc.), have the rest of the group members "poke holes" in the evidence. Afterward, discuss which proofs offered by the person were most persuasive. It may have to do with the number and reliability of the witnesses. Explain that the Bible offers similar evidence. A book like Josh McDowell's *Evidence That Demands a Verdict* can be a big help to those with doubts.

Step 3

To help group members better understand the passages, provide the following background in addition to the suggestions in the session. For the John passage, explain that when Jesus was crucified, His hands and feet were nailed to the cross and that a soldier stuck a spear in His side to make sure that He was dead. That's what caused the holes that Thomas wanted to see and touch. He wanted physical evidence that Jesus' crucified body had really risen. For the Acts passage, explain that Paul took many missionary journeys. In each city he visited, he first went to the Jewish synagogue, where he showed the people that Jesus was the Messiah about whom the Jewish Scriptures (our Old Testament) had prophesied.

Step 5

Group members with little Bible background may have difficulty applying the SCRAM principles because they won't automatically know what the Bible says about various doubts. In fact, they may not even know how to find out what the Bible says. To help them with this problem, choose one or two doubts, such as "I doubt God exists," and show group members some passages that reveal what the Bible says about each doubt. For the "I doubt God exists" example, some possible passages might include Genesis 1:1 ("In the beginning God created . . .") and Exodus 3:14 (in which God says to Moses, "I am who I am"). If possible, bring in some Bible concordances and other resources and briefly demonstrate to your group members how to use them to find various words and topics in the Bible.

Step 1

Use the following game either before or instead of the world records quiz. It will help group members learn more about each other and get them thinking about what makes a statement believable. Divide into two teams. Have group members make up three statements about themselves, two of which are true and one of which is false. Have a player from Team A read his or her statements; then have a player from Team B guess which one is false. If the player guesses correctly, Team B gets a point; if he or she guesses wrong, Team A gets a point. Keep playing until all of the players have read their statements. (If you have a large group, you may want to arrange for several smaller competitions.) Afterward, have group members discuss why they doubted or believed various statements.

Step 5

Close the session with a time of prayer in which group members confess their doubts and ask God's help for belief. You can use all or some of the doubts on Repro Resource 1 or have group members come up with a list of their top ten doubts. Have different volunteers read aloud one of the doubts (from the sheet or your list); then have the group respond with the refrain "Lord, I believe, help my unbelief." End with a time of personal confession of doubts, either having kids pray silently or letting volunteers confess their own doubts aloud. During the prayer time, you may also want to read some of the claims that the Bible makes about God.

Step 3

Instead of having group members describe Thomas, ask for two volunteers to roleplay the event in John 20:24-30. Ask one of the volunteers to play the role of Thomas and the other to play the role of Jesus. The rest of the group members will play other disciples and friends present at the scene. Ask that the characters ad-lib a conversation beyond what is told in the John passage. Suggest that the group members playing disciples and friends contribute to the skit by reacting to Thomas's doubt.

Step 5

Ask group members to select one item from "Dozens-O-Doubts" (Repro Resource 1). Have those who are interested in discussing the same items meet together and talk about how to help each other implement the SCRAM method with that doubt.

Step 1

Play "Sentinel" to help guys test their ability to determine whether someone's telling the truth. Have group members form two teams. One team will be the sentinels; the other will be the challengers. Give each of the challengers a slip of paper that says either "friend" or "foe." When a challenger approaches a sentinel, the sentinel will say, "Halt. Are you friend or foe?" The challenger will reply, "Friend." The sentinel must determine if the challenger is telling the truth. The sentinel gets a point for letting friends pass and for refusing foes. The challenger gets a point if the sentry lets a foe pass or refuses a friend. After all the challengers have played, switch roles. Wrap up the activity by discussing how the sentinels made their decisions. Did they guess? Did they look for certain clues? On what did they base their doubts?

Step 4

Before discussing the principles for dealing with doubts, help group members think about the criteria they already use for determining whether or not someone is trustworthy. Give each group member an index card and have him think of a hero or a person he respects and who he thinks can be believed. Instruct group members to make "hero" cards (modeled after baseball cards). On one side, they should write the hero's/heroine's name (and draw a picture of him or her, if they like). On the other side, they should list the person's "stats," the things that make this person believable. When they are finished, have volunteers share their cards. Discuss what causes us to trust people. (It may include their characters, examples of things they've said that proved true, their reputations, their positions, etc.) Use these ideas to help group members see the trustworthiness of the Bible's claims and of the counsel of other believers.

Step 1

Play the following game to get group members thinking about the issues of believability and trust. Have group members form a circle. Choose a volunteer ("It") to stand in the center of the circle. While "It" closes his or her eyes, the people in the circle should pass around a marble (keeping both hands in front of them, palms down), trying to keep its location hidden. After 30 seconds or so, have "It" give a warning, then open his or her eyes and try to guess who has the marble. The people in the circle should do all they can to trick "It," but they must keep the marble moving. If "It" guesses correctly, the person caught becomes "It." If "It" guesses wrong, he or she has to try again. Afterward, discuss the difficulty of trying to decide who to believe and who to doubt.

Step 4

Briefly introduce each of the SCRAM principles, but don't pause for review. Instead, use a more interesting method of helping kids familiarize themselves with the principles. Have group members form teams of three or four. Instruct each team to come up with a creative and/or humorous presentation of the five SCRAM principles. One team may choose to present the principles in rap form. ("Yo, listen everybody, to our plan. It's got five parts, and they spell out 'Scram' . . .") Another team may put the principles to a TV theme song—*Gilligan's Island,* for instance. ("Just sit right back and you'll hear a tale, a tale of a plan called 'Scram'. . . . There's 'Seek God's help'; 'Call it what it is'; 'Read what the Bi-i-ble says'; 'Ask people you trust'; 'Make a de-cis-ion, and move on'—and your doubts will scram.") Other teams may use poems, jokes, limericks, cheers, cartoons, etc. They may keep the original words or rewrite the principles in their own words—whichever is more conducive to their creativity. When everyone is finished, have each team make its presentation.

Step 1

Bring in several tabloid newspapers, such as the *National Enquirer.* Have group members form two teams. Give each team several tabloids. Instruct each team to choose three headlines from the newspapers and then make up a fourth headline. Each team will then try to guess which of its opponent's headlines is made up. Play several rounds. Afterward, discuss how group members determined which headlines were made up. Use this activity to lead into a discussion of how we determine whether to believe something or not.

Step 5

Here's a way for kids to apply two of the SCRAM principles ("read what the Bible says" and "ask someone you trust") to some of their doubts. Have group members form teams. Assign one doubt to each team. (You might want to take a poll to figure out the top five doubts of your group members and then assign those doubts.) Provide the teams with tape recorders or video cameras. Instruct each team to make a public-service message to help kids overcome the doubt assigned to the team. Encourage the teams to include relevant Bible verses and "expert opinions" or "endorsements" in their messages. When they are finished, play and discuss the messages.

Step 1

Depending on the amount of time you have, you may need to either shorten this step by reading only half of the records or skip the step entirely and begin the session with the "Dozens-O-Doubts" sheet in Step 2. If you skip the step, you might want to be prepared to open the session with an anecdote about a time you (or someone you know of) doubted something that turned out to be true. Then, if you have time, you could ask one or two group members to share similar anecdotes.

Step 4

If you're short on time, you may need to condense the activities in this step. Here are some suggestions. Don't ask kids what they would tell a pesky brother or sister and don't have them shout "scram." Instead, distribute Repro Resource 2 and list each of the five steps. You can save additional time by not pausing to review the steps. By presenting this information quickly, you will give kids more time to apply these principles to their own doubts in Step 5.

Step 1

Here are some other records that may interest city teens.
1. Three New York City youths rode nearly 232 miles on the subway in almost 30 hours. (Real.)
2. Michael Jordan once leaped 40 feet to slam from midcourt. (Fake.)
3. The tallest hairstyle for a woman stood eight feet high. (Real.)
4. The tallest (8' 3/4") **and smallest** (28.3") **living persons are both of African heritage.** (Real.)
5. The biggest-selling rap song of all time is "End of the Road" by Boyz II Men. (Fake—It's not a rap song.)
6. Wilt Chamberlain once scored 100 points in one basketball game. (Real.)
7. In 1972, a fourteen-year-old weight lifter in Miami lifted 762 pounds. (Fake.)

Step 3

For the conversation activity that begins this step, you may want to use a scenario other than "the best vacation" the person ever had. Many urban teens never leave the city, and a "vacation" is an almost-foreign concept to them. Instead, you might want to ask the person to talk about the best day he or she ever had.

Step 4
Since some high schoolers might find the SCRAM acrostic "beneath" them, skip the beginning of the step—especially the part in which kids yell "scram." Skip the sheet as well. Instead, have group members form teams. Instruct each team to come up with a list of steps for handling doubts. After five minutes, have the teams share their lists. List all of the steps on the board as they are named. Afterward, you may want to supplement the teams' ideas with the SCRAM principles (though not by that name).

Step 5
If you skipped the SCRAM principles in Step 4, don't have kids write "SCRAM" over their main doubt. Instead, after they have highlighted their top three doubts, have them choose the main doubt they want to face. Then, on the back of Repro Resource 1, have them make a list of the steps they can take to face (and perhaps overcome) this doubt. Encourage them to use the different strategies developed in Step 4.

Step 4
Help your sixth graders be more specific with the R and A on "The SCRAM Doubt-Removal System" (Repro Resource 2). After you write in the acrostic "Read what the Bible says" and "Ask people you trust," talk about ways to find out where to look in the Bible for specific information. On another section of the board, make a list of some Bible references, such as concordances, Bible dictionaries, and the names of a few specific books. Also write the names of some knowledgeable people in your church who would be receptive to a personal discussion with your group members.

Step 5
Practice the "Call it what it is" step by asking each of your sixth graders to select one of the doubts from Repro Resource 1 to discuss. Distribute pencils and small pieces of paper. Instruct group members to write the number of the doubt they chose on the paper. Collect the papers and put them in a small container. Then draw the slips one at a time, and spend some time discussing the doubts that are identified.

Date Used:

Approx.
Time

Step 1: The "I Doubt It" Game _____
o Large Group
o Fellowship & Worship
o Mostly Guys
o Extra Fun
o Media
o Short Meeting Time
o Urban
Things needed:

Step 2: Dozens-O-Doubts _____
o Small Group
o Heard It All Before
Things needed:

Step 3: Doubting Thomas _____
o Extra Action
o Large Group
o Little Bible Background
o Mostly Girls
o Urban
Things needed:

Step 4: SCRAM _____
o Extra Action
o Heard It All Before
o Mostly Guys
o Extra Fun
o Short Meeting Time
o Combined Junior High/High School
o Sixth Grade
Things needed:

Step 5: Pick a Doubt _____
o Small Group
o Little Bible Background
o Fellowship & Worship
o Mostly Girls
o Media
o Combined Junior High/High School
o Sixth Grade
Things needed:

2 What Does It Cost and What Do I Get?

YOUR GOALS FOR THIS SESSION:

C h o o s e   o n e   o r   m o r e

☐ To help kids understand the cost and benefits of following Christ.

☐ To help kids realize that their commitment to Christ should be a whole-hearted commitment.

☐ To help kids make a decision to follow Christ out of commitment to Him.

☐ Other _____
_____

Your Bible Base:

Mark 10:17-31
Luke 14:25-35
John 15:18-21

Survival Quest

(Needed: Copies of Repro Resource 3, poster board or newsprint, markers, pencils)

In this fun team effort, group members will have to make some choices about the necessities of life. Divide group members into teams of three or four. Pass out copies of "Survival Quest" (Repro Resource 3) to each team. Also give each team a couple of pieces of poster board or newsprint and markers.

Go over the situation at the top of the sheet together; then tell teams they have ten minutes to decide what supplies to take. Have them draw or write out their strategies for survival.

After a few minutes, interrupt with this scenario: **BOOM! There goes the plane. Believe it or not, things have gotten worse. Without enough water and food, your chances of survival are slim. There's no way you can make it to the town. Your only three concerns should be staying as cool as possible during the day, collecting as much water as possible, and signaling passing search planes.**

With this turn of events, which supplies do you absolutely need, and which ones can you leave behind?

Have teams rethink their strategies, and if necessary, come up with different plans of action. When kids have finished, regroup and give teams a chance to present their strategies. Keep track of which supplies are taken, and which are left behind. You might want to take a group vote on the best strategy for survival.

Use the following information to supplement your discussion of which supplies would be useful and which would be useless.

Here are the items that would come in handy:

• *Plastic raincoat*—Could be used for collecting dew at night.

• *Plastic canteen*—Could be used to store the dew where it won't evaporate as you ration it out.

• *Bag of oranges*—Could supply additional water and energy.

• *Hand mirror*—Could be used for signaling planes during the day.

• *Flashlight*—Could be used for signaling planes at night.

Here are the items that could be left behind:

• *Can of lighter fluid*—What would you burn? What would you light it with?

• *Map and compass*—You'd die trying to get to a town that's 500 miles away.

• *Rattlesnake serum*—There are no rattlesnakes in the Sahara.

• *Loaded handgun*—There's nothing to shoot.

• *"Acme Desert Weasel Bait" and* Acme's 101 Ways to Prepare Desert Weasel—That terrible Acme company lives off the stupidity of tourists who don't know there's no such thing as a desert weasel.

• *Jumbo bag of Fritos*—They'd dry you out and make you more thirsty.

Say something like: **Being a follower of Jesus Christ is kind of like this survival quest. We have to make choices about what things to give up—like the Fritos and the Acme desert weasel books—in order to live the right way. There are other things God gives us—like hand mirrors and raincoats—that we may not always see the advantage of having right away, but are exactly what we need for living. In fact, if we try to make it on our own, we'll die. We need a rescuer like Jesus.**

STEP 2

Plus and Minus

(Needed: Index cards with plus signs and minus signs written on them)

For this activity, you'll need several index cards. Before the meeting, draw plus signs on half of the cards and minus signs on the other half. Have everyone sit in a circle, and then randomly hand out the cards to kids.

Explain: **If you have a plus sign on your card, think of one plus about being a Christian and write it on your card. If you have a minus sign, write one negative thing about being a Christian.**

Some of your kids might feel weird writing down negative things about being a Christian. If this is the case, have them write what *other* kids think are some of the negative things about being a Christian.

Let your kids work for a couple of minutes. Then ask someone who has a positive sign on his or her card to read one of the advantages, and toss the card in the middle of the circle. Others with the same response should rip up their cards. Do the same thing for someone with a negative sign. Go back and forth between the advantages and disadvantages, even if kids run out of cards to toss. When all the cards are in the middle, count up the pluses and the minuses. At this point, it's all right if

OPTIONS

LARGE GROUP

HEARD IT ALL BEFORE

LITTLE BIBLE BACKGROUND

MOSTLY GUYS

MEDIA

SIXTH GRADE

the negatives outnumber the positives. The positive group may have had a hard time coming up with advantages other than "going to heaven." If kids give vague, general responses such as "too many rules," press them to be more specific.

Afterward, say: **When you follow Christ, you have to count up the pluses and minuses, or the costs involved in following Him.**

The Price Is Right

(Needed: Bibles, slips of paper with Scripture references written on them, a ten-dollar bill, a five-dollar bill, a one-dollar bill, pieces of green construction paper with dollar amounts written on them [optional])

If you can, bring a ten-, a five-, and a one-dollar bill to this session. Or, if you're not feeling wealthy, write these same dollar amounts on three separate sheets of green construction paper.

Have group members move back into their teams from Step 1 or form three new groups. Give each team a slip of paper with one of the following passages to read. Explain that the teams are to come up with one or two "costs" involved in following Jesus.

Here are the passages:
• Mark 10:17-31
• Luke 14:25-35
• John 15:18-21

Give the teams a few minutes to work; then go over their findings. To do this, ask each group to describe what was going on in its passage and to name at least one cost involved in following Jesus. Also hand the reporting group the ten-, five-, and one-dollar bills (or green construction paper).

Explain: **Hold up the ten-dollar bill and call out "Too high," if you think the cost was too high. Hold up the one-dollar bill if you think the cost was too low. Hold up the five-dollar bill if you think the cost was just right.**

Give each group a minute to decide which amount to hold up and to explain the choice.

Use the following information to supplement your discussion of these hard teachings of Jesus.

Mark 10:17-31—This is the story of the rich young man (or ruler as he's described in Luke 18:18). The young man thought he could earn salvation, but Jesus taught that it was a gift to be received. Even though the young man sincerely kept the law, it was still an external kind of obedience. Jesus obviously cared for the young man and knew he was sincere; but He also wanted the man to realize the depth of God's commandments. Jesus' commandment to go and sell everything and give it to the poor may not apply to every single Christian; but in this case, the young man's major problem was his wealth—and it kept him from following Jesus.

Cost involved in following Jesus: Being willing to give up everything.

Luke 14:25-35—This passage describes the cost of being a disciple. In verse 26, Jesus used exaggeration to make His point: A person must love Him even more than immediate family members. The phrase "carry his cross" communicates the total commitment involved in following Christ. Since the cross was a symbol of death, that commitment includes dying for Christ's sake—but it also means self-denial, complete loyalty, and a willing obedience. Jesus doesn't want a blind, everything-is-going-to-be-wonderful-now commitment. Just as a builder estimates the cost or a king evaluates his military strength, a person must consider what Jesus expects of His followers—total commitment to Him.

Costs involved in following Jesus: Relationships with people can't be more important than Christ; suffering; self-denial; total commitment to God.

John 15:18-21—This passage contains some of Jesus' parting words to His disciples. Jesus reminds His followers that if the world (that is, the human system that opposes God's purposes) hates them, it's because the world hated Him first. Christians don't belong to the world's system anymore. They have new life in Christ and belong to Him. So guess what? People will treat Christians the way they treated Christ. But remember, it's a sign of belonging to Christ.

Costs involved in following Christ: Being unpopular and hated; persecution.

After all the groups have shared, say: **For every cost we talked about, we could have said that it was too high. Why do you think the cost in following Jesus is so high?** (Jesus wants to be sure that we are following Him completely. Our relationship with Christ has to be the most important relationship we have. He wants us to be ready to give up everything for Him, and even be prepared to suffer for His sake.)

To help kids understand the total commitment Christ demands, say: **Suppose you liked someone who really liked you too, but he or she only wanted to be your boyfriend or girlfriend fifty percent of the time. The other fifty percent of the time, he or she wanted to someone else's girlfriend or boyfriend. How would you feel about this person's commitment to you?**

As kids describe their feelings, mention that a halfway commitment usually means no real commitment at all.

Explain: **The same thing can be said about our choice to follow Christ. We either do it all the way, or not at all. It's not a halfway commitment. That's why Jesus wants His followers to count the cost, and choose to follow Him one hundred percent. We've been talking about some serious stuff, but there are some pretty good trade-offs involved in following Christ.**

STEP 4

Let's Make a Trade

(Needed: Four assorted sizes of boxes, wrapping paper, slips of paper, envelopes)

Before the session, collect four assorted sizes of boxes (for example, a shoe box, a photocopy paper box, a grocery store box, and a shirt box). For each box, cover one side of it with wrapping paper (or some substitute). Also label the boxes 1, 2, 3, and 4.

On the opposite side of the box, write one of the benefits of following Christ. Here are some sample benefits you might want to use:
- Forgiveness—You don't have to live with a guilty conscience.
- Eternal life—You don't have to worry about death.
- Peace—God is in charge and is good even in bad times.
- Love and acceptance
- Help with problems

Next, write on slips of paper some of the "benefits" of not following Christ. For example:
- Popularity with a lot of different people
- Freedom to do whatever you want
- Don't have to go to church all the time
- No pressure to act a certain way
- Life is good just the way it is—no reason to change

Put these slips of paper in envelopes.

Instead of coming up with new benefits, you might want to reuse the negative cards from Step 2. If you do, just hand out the cards, without the envelopes.

To wrap up the session, ask for four volunteers to play "Let's Make a Trade." Hand out the envelopes and tell kids to open them and read

what's inside. Meanwhile, set up the boxes, with the wrapped side facing your kids.

Play this part as a Monty Hall clone from the old game show "Let's Make a Deal." Explain how the trade works.

Each of you has one "advantage" of not being a Christian. Inside these boxes are some of the advantages of following Christ. So, would you like to trade what's in your envelope for what's behind Box #1, Box #2, Box #3, or Box #4?

Get the other kids to yell out which boxes the volunteers should choose. When a choice has been made, have the volunteer come up to the box, turn it around, and read the advantage to the rest of the group.

As a group, talk about the trade-offs. Ask kids what they would have to give up and what they would receive in return. For example, if a person traded freedom for forgiveness, he or she might not be able to do certain things anymore. But, when he or she blows it, God will forgive him or her—and the person doesn't have to live with a guilty conscience.

Say: **As Jesus said, each of us has to count the cost in following Him. Are the trade-offs worth it? I think so.**

Encourage kids to make a decision to follow Christ wholeheartedly. Close in prayer, thanking God for all the benefits of following Christ.

Survival Quest

You and your tour group were flying in a small airplane over the Sahara Desert when your engine caught fire. You made an emergency landing in the middle of nowhere. You see nothing but sand in every direction. According to the map, the nearest town is about 500 miles away. The temperature is 111 degrees. Once you land, you discover that fuel is leaking near the flames, and the plane will explode any second.

You have to act fast before the plane goes up in flames, so you grab an armload (five items) of supplies from the plane. All the passengers are OK, with only minor cuts and scrapes—except for one, who appears to have broken a leg.

What supplies would you take from the plane? Circle five items from the following list:

- a plastic raincoat

- a can of lighter fluid

- a map of the region

- a compass

- a vile of rattlesnake serum

- a flashlight

- a loaded handgun

- an empty plastic canteen

- a can labeled "Acme Desert Weasel Bait"

- a small hand mirror

- a book titled *Acme's 101 Ways to Prepare Desert Weasel*

- a bag with three oranges in it

- a jumbo bag of Fritos Corn Chips

AS A GROUP, PLAN WHAT YOU'LL DO NEXT.

Step 1

Adapt the opening "survival quest" activity to use as a trading game for your group members. Before the session, you'll need to prepare several index cards, each with one of the supplies from the plane (in the story) written on it. If necessary, write each supply item on two or more cards. You'll need two cards per group member. As group members arrive, distribute the cards. Then read the scenario from Repro Resource 3. Have group members look at the supplies written on their cards and decide whether those supplies would be useful or not. If not, they should trade cards with others, trying to get two useful items. The catch to this activity is that some of the most useful items (like the plastic raincoat) are not obviously useful. So some group members may trade away useful items without realizing it. After a few minutes, reveal which items are useful. Follow up the activity with the comments at the end of the step.

Step 4

Get kids actively involved in examining trade-offs with the following activity. Have the group brainstorm a list of the advantages of being a Christian and a list of the advantages of not being a Christian. Give everyone a slip of paper and a pencil. Have half of your group members write down one advantage of being a Christian and the other half write down one advantage of not being a Christian. When they are finished writing, give them five minutes for free-for-all trading. Instruct them to try to get the best advantage possible. Afterward, discuss some of the trades. Ask: **What do you trade? What did you get? Why did you make the trade?** You may find that the kids who wrote advantages of not being a Christian get stuck with them. Discuss why that happened.

Step 1

Help your group members get to know each other better by having them answer a series of questions about trade-offs. Have group members form a circle. One at a time, have each person answer this question: **What would you have to get in return to convince you to give up eating sweets for a month?** After everyone has answered, try another question. Here are some other questions you might use: **What would you have to get in return to convince you to give up television for a month? What would you have to get in return to convince you to give up your Saturday nights for a month?** Afterward, explain that in this session you will discuss some of the costs and benefits of being a Christian.

Step 4

Encourage group members to choose one thing they could give up to follow Jesus more wholeheartedly. Begin by having them list various things that they could give up. If they have trouble coming up with ideas, get them started with some of the following suggestions: give up sleep so they have more time for devotions; give up songs, television shows, or movies that aren't God-honoring; give up some of their relaxation time to help others; etc. When the list is finished, have group members choose one idea from the list to apply to their lives. Then ask each person to share what he or she chose. Wrap up the session by having group members pray for the people to their left. They may pray either aloud or silently—whichever they would be most comfortable with.

Step 2

If uou have too many kids to do the plus/minus index cards, you'll need to modify the activity. Have group members form teams of five. Assign half of the teams to come up with as many advantages of being a Christian as they can; assign the other teams to come up with as many disadvantages of being a Christian as they can. After five minutes or so, have the teams share their ideas. Make a master list on the board, using plus and minus columns.

Step 4

Review the lists you made in Step 2 of the advantages and disadvantages of being a Christian. If there aren't many advantages on the list, supplement them with the suggestions in the guide (forgiveness, eternal life, peace, love and acceptance, and help with problems). Then have group members form teams of four or five. Give each team ten index cards. Instruct the teams to write down five advantages and five disadvantages (one per card). Then have the teams arrange the advantages and disadvantages in pairs according to which ones would be worthwhile trade-offs. (For instance, the "love and acceptance" of being a Christian would be worth giving up the luxury of "not having as many rules to live by" as a non-Christian.) After a few minutes, have each team share and explain some of its matches.

Step 2

There is a tendency among many Christians, at least in the United States, to emphasize the benefits of Christianity and say little about the costs. Your kids may have heard the benefits all of their lives. Before thinking about them more, they need to be challenged with the costs. After all, as Christians we're not called to an easy life. Have your group members come up with a list of reasons *not* to be Christians. Focusing only on the negative may shock them enough to get them thinking. You might even wait until Step 4 to introduce the advantages of being a Christian.

Step 4

Help your group members apply the Bible teaching of Step 3 to their own situations. Have group members form teams. Instruct each team to rewrite the Bible passages using modern examples for junior high students. (They could make them into skits.) Have the teams concentrate on one of the following questions: **What are you willing to give up? Who are you willing to give up? How much are you willing to give up?** For example, in one rewrite, Jesus might tell a young person to give away his or her Nintendo. After a few minutes, have the teams share their rewrites (or perform their skits); then talk about what Jesus might give in return.

Step 2

Non-Christians and even young Christians might have difficulty coming up with advantages of being a Christian. After they've brainstormed a list of the disadvantages of being a Christian, you might want to suggest some advantages, such as eternal life, the comfort of knowing that God is always with you, the knowledge that God will forgive you if you mess up, etc. Be honest about the costs (or disadvantages) of being a Christian, but try to get group members to see that the benefits outweigh the costs.

Step 4

Expand the discussion in this section to challenge your group members' thinking, especially if you have non-Christians in your group. After each trade-off is made in the game, get kids to discuss whether or not they think the trade was worthwhile. Try to create an atmosphere in which kids feel safe to express their views, even if you disagree with them. Try not to attack or judge their answers, especially if they think that being a non-Christian is more advantageous. After discussing the trade-offs, you might have kids think about what's wrong with some of the "benefits" of being a non-Christian.

Step 1

Begin the session with the following icebreaker. Have group members pair off. Instruct the members of each pair to sit on the floor back-to-back, knees bent, elbows linked. Then have them stand up together. (Make sure the pairs have room to move.) With a little give and take, they should master this activity. After they do, have them try it in groups of three, four, and so on, as you have time. You may want to follow it up by discussing the give and take necessary to accomplish the task.

Step 4

After discussing the trade-offs, encourage group members to think about what things they might give up to help them become more wholeheartedly committed to Christ. Encourage them to think about different areas of their lives, such as their use of time, their bodies, friends, entertainment, thoughts, etc. Distribute slips of paper and pencils. Have each person write one thing he or she will do to be more committed. Wrap up the session with prayer for these commitments. You could have kids pray aloud with the whole group or have them pair up and pray for their partners. You may even just want to have a time of silent prayer. Close the prayer time by thanking God that the benefits of following Christ outweigh the costs.

Step 3

Instruct the teams to list the "costs" on the board as they work through their assigned passages. After the teams have reported, ask group members if they know of other "costs" involved in serving Christ. Have them add any they can think of to the list. Then ask: **When you consider the "costs" involved in following Christ, does your commitment become stronger? Why or why not?**

Step 4

After playing "Let's Make a Trade," talk about the benefits of being a Christian. Ask group members to choose two benefits they would use in talking to a friend who is not a Christian. Have them explain why they would talk about those benefits.

Step 1

As an alternative to the survival quest, have your group member "buy" a car. Bring in advertisements for four different kinds of cars: a basic economy car, a luxury sedan, a family car, and a sports car. (If you can't find the ads, you could make up your own, giving the make and model, the price, and the features that are included in the price.) Have your group members examine the ads and decide which is the best buy. (They could do this individually, in pairs, or in teams.) Then have them discuss their decisions: which they thought was the best deal and why. (There will certainly be some interesting arguing.) Next, discuss the decision-making process. What factors did they take into consideration? (It will probably have a lot to do with costs versus benefits.)

Step 2

Before discussing the advantages and disadvantages of being a Christian, get your group members to think about the advantages and disadvantages of commitments in general. For example, you might ask: **What does it mean to belong to a sports team? What might you have to give up? What do you get in return?** You might also have group members consider the advantages and disadvantages of having a girlfriend, being in the youth group, and being part of a family. Afterward, talk about the advantages and disadvantages of being a Christian.

Step 1

Begin the session by having group members play a game of crab soccer (or a similarly goofy game). To play, you'll need an open space and a beach ball. Have group members form two teams. Set up some chairs as goals. Explain that the players have to "walk" crab style—on their hands and feet with their backs toward the floor—during the game. (Watch out for rug burns!) Use the game to introduce a discussion of what it means to be committed to a team. Ask: **What do you give up when you're part of a team? What do you get in return?** Explain that this session will focus on the costs and benefits of a commitment to Christ.

Step 4

In keeping with the idea of trade-offs, add this twist to serving refreshments. Arrange to have five different kinds of refreshments—perhaps a drink, cookies, brownies, popcorn, and cupcakes. Divide your group into five teams. Give one kind of refreshment to each team. Let each team divide its food among its members (for example, five bags of popcorn per person). Then have group members trade their goods to get things that they want.

Step 2

Before the session have different adults and kids tape-record statements that express the advantages or disadvantages of being a Christian. For example, someone might say, "Being a Christian is great because you know you'll go to heaven" or "Christians have to follow a bunch of rules." Try to get at least five statements of each type. During the session, play the tape for your group members. As you discuss the statements, ask group members how common they think these views are and to what extent they agree with the comments. Also, you might ask group members to add some statements of their own.

Step 4

Play a popular song that disparages Christianity and praises an alternative way of living. After listening to the song, discuss it with questions like the following: **What negative things does the song say about being a Christian? What positive things does it say about not being a Christian? To what extent do you think the song is right? What is the song missing? What is the real trade-off?** If you can't think of a contemporary song, you might play "Only the Good Die Young" by Billy Joel. In the song, he makes fun of a Catholic girl for believing in heaven and for choosing to remain a virgin.

Step 1

To save time, you may need to skip this step or condense it. You can do the latter by not breaking into teams. Instead, distribute "Survival Quest" (Repro Resource 3), have the kids read the situation, and give them a few minutes to circle five items on the list. Have several volunteers share the items they chose; then discuss as a group which of the choices were best and why.

Step 4

Condense this step by eliminating the "Let's Make a Trade" game. Instead, have group members brainstorm a list of the benefits of being a Christian and a list of the benefits of not being a Christian. Discuss the two lists in terms of trade-offs. Have the kids pair off the benefits in terms of opposites. Which side cancels out the other? Encourage group members to see that we gain more in being Christians than we lose.

Step 1

As an alternative situation, have your group members imagine that they are on a subway car a mile underground when it suddenly veers off the main track and onto an old one that hasn't been used for sixty years. As the subway shudders on the uncharted, unused, and tattered tracks, the driver announces "We're going to crash!" BOOM! After the crash, the subway car is in total darkness—but at least everyone is safe. You are now four miles underground. No one knows where you are, including you. To add insult to injury, the radio is broken and it's 25° Fahrenheit outside the car. Almost all of the items on Repro Resource 3 are found on this car, with these substitutions:
• roach spray (instead of rattlesnake serum)
• a fifty-foot rope (instead of a can labeled "Acme Desert Weasel Bait")
• ten old, moldy blankets (instead of a book titled *Acme's 101 Ways to Prepare Desert Weasel*).

Step 4

When city teens say the cost of being a Christian in the city can be high, it's true. The result can be death itself. Have each of your group members add up on a piece of paper the cost he or she is *willing* to pay for living a Christian lifestyle. Instruct group members to make four columns on the sheet, labeled as follows: (1) Emotional Cost—what will happen to my state of mind; (2) Social Cost—what will happen to my relationship with friends and family; (3) Physical Cost—what will happen to my body; (4) Spiritual Cost—what will happen to my soul. Then, under each category, group members should write a number from 1 to 10 (with 10 being the highest), indicating how far they are willing to go for Jesus in that area. When they're finished, have them add up their costs. Use the following table in grading the scores: 4-10 —bankrupt; 11-20—more safe than sorry; 21-30—getting faithful; 31-40—high spiritual value.

Step 3

With a combined group, you may want to make the following adjustments to this step. First, eliminate the part in which kids wave money, since it probably won't go over well with high schoolers. Second, if possible, divide the teams according to age. Assign John 15:18-21 to your high school students. Given their more developed analytical skills, they will be better equipped to handle the fairly difficult concepts in this passage.

Step 4

Continue with the "cost" theme developed in Step 3. Although the costs to junior highers and high schoolers are fairly similar, they may not seem that way to the kids. If possible, have group members form teams according to age (with high schoolers together and junior highers together). Instruct the teams to brainstorm some of the costs of being a Christian in junior high or in high school. Encourage them to think about areas of their lives such as dating, going to parties, being cool, and being up on certain movies or music. After the teams come up with costs, have them brainstorm benefits. Then have them choose a cost and a benefit from their lists and make up a slogan, showing how the benefit outweighs the cost. For example, "It's better to be a Christian geek in high school than a cool goat for eternity." After a few minutes, have the teams share their lists and slogans.

Step 2

Some sixth graders may have difficulty describing what they consider the positive or negative things about being a Christian. Instead of distributing index cards to individuals, give one card to a team of two or three kids. Ask the team members to work together to decide what information they want to write on their card in response to the "+" or "–" sign on it. Explain that the information they write will be anonymous; after they've written on the card, they can toss it into the circle without reading it aloud. After all the cards have been completed, read them to the group; then discuss them together.

Step 3

Read through the Bible passages together as a group instead of having your sixth graders work in teams. Write the conclusions about the costs involved on the board. After the three conclusions have been listed, have your group members use the money to vote on the "cost" of following Jesus.

Date Used:

Approx. Time

Step 1: Survival Quest _____
o Extra Action
o Small Group
o Fellowship & Worship
o Mostly Guys
o Extra Fun
o Short Meeting Time
o Urban
Things needed:

Step 2: Plus and Minus _____
o Large Group
o Heard It All Before
o Little Bible Background
o Mostly Guys
o Media
o Sixth Grade
Things needed:

Step 3: The Price Is Right _____
o Mostly Girls
o Combined Junior High/High School
o Sixth Grade
Things needed:

Step 4: Let's Make a Trade _____
o Extra Action
o Small Group
o Large Group
o Heard It All Before
o Little Bible Background
o Fellowship & Worship
o Mostly Girls
o Extra Fun
o Media
o Short Meeting Time
o Urban
o Combined Junior High/High School
Things needed:

3 Accepted by God, Rejected by Others

YOUR GOALS FOR THIS SESSION:

Choose one or more

☐ To help group members realize commitment to Christ will sometimes mean that we act differently.

☐ To help group members understand which of their beliefs are important enough to risk rejection for.

☐ To help group members take risks for Jesus, knowing that He understands their rejection.

☐ Other _____

Your Bible Base:

Matthew 3:1-12
Luke 3:1-20; 6:22, 23

STEP 1

Invasion

(Needed: Copies of Repro Resource 4, pencils, drawing paper, markers)

Before the session, you'll need to cut apart several copies of "Aliens!" (Repro Resource 4). To begin the meeting, divide kids into five teams. (Teams may be as small as two people.) Then read aloud the following scenario.

Last night a huge spaceship landed in a field outside the city, and alien creatures stepped off. Our city has been over-run with these creatures. They're trying to blend in with humans in restaurants, stores, malls, and movie theaters. This is a total joke because they don't blend in at all! Not only do they look different, they act completely different. Your job, as members of the "Alien Descriptor Task Force," is to describe the aliens to everyone. Here are your assignments. Distribute one or two assignment slips to each team.

After about five minutes, have each team appoint a spokesperson to report its discoveries to the rest of the group.

After all teams have reported, ask: **Based on the descriptions we've just heard of these aliens, how do you think earthlings will react to them?**

OPTIONS

SMALL GROUP

LITTLE BIBLE BACKGROUND

FELLOWSHIP & WORSHIP

MOSTLY GUYS

EXTRA FUN

MEDIA

SHORT MEETING TIME

JR. HIGH / HIGH SCHOOL COMBINED

STEP 2

Alien Behavior

(Needed: Costumes and props as needed for characters)

For this step, you'll need to collect some costumes and props to portray the following characters:

• Obnoxious Oliver/Olivia—the Christian who crams religion down everyone's throat. This character is totally obnoxious and rude.

• Bigoted Bob/Babs—the Christian who's convinced that he or she has the corner on God's truth, and everyone else is wrong. This character is intolerant, insensitive, and impatient.

   • Authentic Andy/Amanda—the Christian who truly wants to live for Christ. This character accepts other people, but takes a stand on important issues.

If you don't want to play all three characters yourself, get some other people to help you. Use your imagination and creativity in portraying these characters. Bring in props such as a huge Bible or nerdy-looking clothes.

You could play Obnoxious Oliver/Olivia like the Church Lady from "Saturday Night Live." You could play Bigoted Bob/Babs like a Christian Archie Bunker from "All in the Family." You could play Authentic Andy/ Amanda like some of your junior high kids who truly love the Lord. The subject matter is how each character lets other people know that he or she is a Christian, and how he or she acts around people who may not know the Lord.

To introduce the activity, say: **Did you know that the Bible describes Christians as aliens and strangers? We didn't land in a field in a spaceship, but as God's people we may not always fit in with everyone else. But you have to wonder if some Christians don't fit in because of their own doing, not because of Christ's.**

One at a time, introduce the three characters to your kids. If you're playing all three roles yourself, introduce yourself in character and launch into an award-winning monologue. Turn around to make the character switch. If other people are playing the parts, conduct an interview that would make Barbara Walters proud.

When you've finished, say: **Clap, whistle, and stomp your feet if you think Oliver/Olivia did the best job in letting people know he or she is a Christian.**

Give kids a chance to react.

Clap, whistle, and stomp your feet if you think Bob/Babs did the best job.

Give kids a chance to react.

Clap, whistle, and stomp your feet, if you think Andy/ Amanda did the best job.

Give kids a chance to react.

After declaring a winner, ask: **How do you think people would react to these three different characters and their messages about Christ?** Chances are people would totally ignore the obnoxious and bigoted characters; thus, ignoring their message. People would be more accepting of the authentic, sincere character, but they still might reject his or her message.

We can be as sincere and as nice as we possibly can, but people still might not accept us. Why might this be true?
(Some people just may not believe in God or Jesus. Some people may feel that beliefs are personal and shouldn't be discussed with others.

Some people may think you're trying to change them, and may resist. Some people don't like to hear that they're sinners and need a Savior.)

Alien Prophet

(Needed: Bibles, dried locusts and honey [optional])

[OPTION: Before this session, try to find some edible dried locusts. Check with a wildlife and nature center, a health food store, or the neighborhood entomologist. If you find some, bring them to the meeting, along with some honey. Dare kids to eat the locusts and honey. (If you can't find any, substitute something else that's crunchy, like pork rinds.)]

Ask: **What would you think of a Christian who ate locusts and honey, wore weird clothes, lived alone, and went around town shouting, "Repent!"** (You'd think he or she was crazy. You might make excuses for him or her, telling your non-Christian friends that not every Christian is like that. You might not want this person to come to your church or hang out with you.)

Does anyone know who I just described? Let's hope no one says the pastor of your church! Some of your kids may have figured out that you were describing John the Baptist.

Have kids reassemble into their teams from Step 1. Ask the first three teams to turn in their Bibles to Matthew 3:1-12. Ask the other two teams to look up Luke 3:1-20. Give each team paper and pencils. Instruct the teams to read their assigned passages. As they read, go to each team and assign it the following questions.

Team 1: What do you think John the Baptist looked like? Use your imagination. Remember, he'd lived alone in the wilderness for a while.

Team 2: What was John the Baptist's message? How do you think people reacted to the message and the messenger?

Team 3: Who rejected John the Baptist? Why?

Team 4: Who accepted John the Baptist and listened to his message? Why do you think these people accepted John?

Team 5: What happened to John?

These two passages tell the same story. The Matthew passage describes John the Baptist and states that that his "brood of vipers" comment was directed toward the religious leaders. The Luke passage gives us a clearer picture of his message and his interaction with the crowd.

After about five minutes, have each team go over its answers. Use the following information to supplement the teams' responses.

Team 1—John the Baptist's clothes were made from camel's hair, and he wore a leather belt around his waist. Since he lived in the desert, John the Baptist probably had a permanent tan. His skin may have been as leathery as his belt. He probably had long, tangled hair, and really didn't care how he looked.

Team 2—John the Baptist's message was short and to the point: Repent for the kingdom of God is near. He also warned the religious leaders to "produce fruit in keeping with repentance" (Matthew 3:8). People probably were all across the board in their reactions to John the Baptist; their reactions depended on whether they accepted him or rejected him.

Team 3—The religious leaders and establishment rejected John the Baptist. These were the people who held a lot of power. They didn't think they needed to repent, because they followed the law.

Team 4—The average people who were in the crowd, the tax collectors (who, in Jesus' day, were considered to be among the lowest of the low) and the soldiers—people who didn't have a lot of power or prestige. Perhaps these people knew they needed to repent. They probably had been looking forward to the Messiah's coming and hoped John the Baptist would lead them to the Messiah.

Team 5—John the Baptist sharply criticized Herod and the evil the ruler had done. Herod had divorced his wife to marry his niece, who was already married to his brother. Sounds like an afternoon soap!

Ask if anyone knows the final outcome of John the Baptist's imprisonment. (He was beheaded.)

Wrap up this look at John the Baptist with the following questions.

Do you think John the Baptist did or said anything to create his own problems? (John the Baptist didn't exactly win friends and influence the powerful people by calling them a "brood of vipers" and demanding they produce fruit in keeping with repentance. He was blunt, condemning, and overwhelming. He didn't go out of his way to be nice to people.)

Why do you think John the Baptist was so radical? (He obviously was on a mission from God [that is, the prophet Isaiah told about his coming]. He wanted to be sure people would listen to and understand his message.)

Why do you think John the Baptist didn't care if the religious leaders accepted him? (He wasn't looking for acceptance, but repentance.)

The Bible doesn't really say if John the Baptist felt hurt when he was rejected. Maybe he did, maybe he didn't, but he kept on telling people to turn from their sins and follow God—even if it meant death.

To Die For

(Needed: Copies of Repro Resource 5, pencils)

Who would you die for? Stand up if you'd die for your parents. Pause after each of the following items to allow kids to respond.

Your brothers or sisters?

Your best friend?

Your pet? Kids may be as goofy or as serious as they wish.

Then say: **Let's get a little more serious. You don't have to answer this question aloud, but would you die for your faith in God?**

Pass out pencils and copies of "To Die For" (Repro Resource 5). Read the instructions at the top of the page together. Then give group members about five minutes to complete the sheet.

When everyone has finished, ask: **Did this help you decide which of your beliefs were the most important, to-die-for beliefs?** Call on several kids to tell which beliefs they felt were important, and which ones weren't all that important to them.

If something is important enough to die for, do you think it's worth a little rejection?

Pain of Rejection

(Needed: Bibles, blank paper, markers)

Just for fun, show how you would reject the person sitting next to you. If you need to get things going, suggest these ways: plug one's ears, turn one's back on the person, walk away, or stick one's nose up in the air.

Ask: **Have you ever been rejected or made fun of because of what you believe?** Ask for a few volunteers to share examples.

Then say: **In real life, rejection isn't funny. If we're serious about following Christ, some people might reject us. Believe it or not, Jesus says this kind of rejection is a good thing.**

Have group members look up Luke 6:22, 23. Ask someone to read it aloud.

Then ask: **What's your first reaction to these verses?** Hand out blank paper and markers, and encourage kids to write down the first thing that pops into their heads. At the count of three, have everyone hold up his or her paper.

Say: **Read aloud some of the things other people have written down. Do you agree or disagree with their reactions?** Give kids a minute to express their opinions.

What do you think the word "blessed" means? Some of your kids might suggest the word "happiness." That's true, but the word has a deeper meaning than just happiness. Blessed means having a sense of well-being, because the person trusts God, not the circumstances, for his or her happiness.

Explain: **Everything Jesus described in these verses eventually happened to Him. Jesus understands all about the pain of rejection. That won't magically take away the pain, but you can tell Him exactly how you're feeling when people reject you for His sake.**

Ask kids to close their eyes so they can make a personal decision, without being influenced by anyone.

Say: **I'm going to read three statements. When you hear one that you want to try, raise your left hand. You don't have to choose any of them, but keep your eyes closed. Here are the statements:**

• **I'm willing to take more risks for Jesus.**

• **I'll try not to create my own problems by being an obnoxious Christian.**

• **I'm willing to take a stand on important issues and to back off when the issue isn't all that important.**

Close in prayer, thanking the Lord for understanding the pain of rejection, and asking His help in taking a stand for Him.

OPTIONS

LARGE GROUP

HEARD IT ALL BEFORE

FELLOWSHIP & WORSHIP

MOSTLY GIRLS

MOSTLY GUYS

EXTRA FUN

URBAN

JR. HIGH / HIGH SCHOOL COMBINED

ALiENS!

MOO?

ASSIGNMENT #1

• Draw a picture of how the aliens look.

• How many hands or feet do they have, if any? What about their facial
  characteristics?

ASSIGNMENT #2

• Act out the way the aliens greet people and each other.

• How do they say good-bye?

• Show how they communicate their affection for each other.
  (For instance, humans hold hands. What do the aliens do?)

ASSIGNMENT #3

• Do the aliens make any strange noises? If so, imitate the noises.

• Do they smell like anything in particular? If so, describe the smell.

• Act out a conversation between two aliens. How do they talk? Does anything
  move or make sounds besides their mouths (if they have mouths)?

• How do they sleep? Act out an alien bedtime scene.

ASSIGNMENT #4

• Show what happens when the aliens get angry.

• Show how they express happiness or excitement.

• Act out what they do when they think something is really funny or really sad.

ASSIGNMENT #5

• Draw or describe the foods aliens eat.

• Act out any habits the aliens have that might offend humans or make them
  uncomfortable, but not grossed-out or mad.

TO·DIE·FOR

Read each of the following statements. Next to each one, place a check mark in the box that best describes your commitment to that belief. For numbers 9 and 10, write in two issues of your own that you feel strongly about.

a = I don't believe this at all.

b = I believe this is true, but wouldn't take any grief for it.

c = I'd stick with this if only people I didn't like made fun of me.

d = I'd stick with this even if all my friends made fun of me.

e = I'd stick with this even if it meant physical harm to me.

f = I'd stick with this even if it meant death.

	a	b	c	d	e	f
1. Jesus is God.						
2. Jesus is the only way to heaven.						
3. Premarital sex is wrong.						
4. Getting drunk is a sin.						
5. I'm a Christian.						
6. Abortion is murder.						
7. Not everyone will go to heaven.						
8. Satan is real.						
9						
10.						

Step 2

Rather than acting out the three types of Christians yourself, have your group members do it. Divide them into three teams and assign one of the characters to each team. Write the basic description of the character (from the session) on a sheet of paper for each team. Each team should choose someone to play its character then come up with a monologue or skit "starring" this person. (You may want to bring in a box of props for group members to use for their presentations.) After all of the teams have performed, ask group members to vote on their favorite performance. Then discuss the different approaches to sharing your faith, using the questions in the session.

Step 3

Have group members form five teams. Distribute markers and poster board to each team. Instruct the teams to read their assigned passages and discuss the accompanying questions. (You might want to write the team questions on the board.) Then have each team draw a comic strip based on its passage. The strip should answer the team's question—what John the Baptist looked like, how people might have reacted to him, etc. When the teams are finished, have them display and explain their strips. Continue the discussion with the questions in the session.

Step 1

You will need to modify the "Invasion" game to fit your group's size. Have your group members work in pairs. Allow the pairs to choose among the assignments on Repro Resource 4. (Make sure each pair has a different assignment.)

Step 3

If your group is small, you'll need to modify the Bible study activity to accommodate fewer than five teams. You could do this in one of three ways. (1) You could have group members work in pairs, dividing the verses and questions among the different pairs. (2) You could assign individuals to read the passages and answer the appropriate questions. (3) You could read and study the passages as a group. As an alternate way of studying the passage, you could provide poster board and markers and have group members make a mural of John's life as presented in these passages. The mural could contain various scenes, representing his appearance, his message, and how various people reacted to him.

Step 2

For a large group, you might choose one of the following ways to spice up the presentation of the three types of Christians. (1) Before the session, recruit six volunteers. Divide them into three pairs. Explain that the pairs will be roleplaying interviews. Assign one person in each pair to play one of the characters described in the session (Obnoxious Oliver/Olivia, Bigoted Bob/Babs, Authentic Andy Amanda). The other person in each pair will play the interviewer. Instruct each pair to come up with a two-minute interview in which the character can show his or her personality. (2) Ask for four volunteers to roleplay a talk show. One person will play the host of the show; the other three will each play one of the characters described in the session. To begin the roleplay, the host should introduce each character and let each make a few remarks to reveal his or her personality. Then the host should introduce a general topic and ask the guests to comment on it. For instance, the host might ask, "What do you think about _____?" (It could be any controversial issue.) "What would you say to the president [or some other highly visible person] about this topic?"

Step 5

To facilitate honest and open discussion, have group members form teams of three or four for the beginning activities in this step (discussing times in which they have been rejected; responding to Luke 6:22, 23; and reading and discussing others' reaction to those verses). Reassemble the large group to discuss what "blessed" means.

HEARD IT ALL BEFORE

LITTLE BIBLE BACKGROUND

FELLOWSHIP & WORSHIP

Step 3

It's probably quite easy for your young people to side with John the Baptist, the "rebel" outsider. It's also probably easy to overlook the fact that he condemned the religious establishment. Challenge your kids to think about ways in which they belong to the "religious establishment" of today. Also challenge them to think of what a modern-day John the Baptist might say. Then, after they've read the passages and briefly shared their comments, have group members form teams. Instruct the teams to make up their own versions of a modern-day prophet. The teams should emphasize the prophet's appearance and message, and the response of people in your church and/or youth group to this prophet. After a few minutes, have the teams share their ideas.

Step 5

Expand the discussion of Luke 6:22, 23, challenging group members to think about what it means if they aren't rejected for Christ's sake. Point out that part of the blessing of being persecuted is that it's a sign that we're truly following Christ and consequently receiving the same treatment He did. Ask: **If you haven't been rejected for your Christianity, what does that say about the quality of your commitment?** Help your group members see that following Christ requires more than *knowing* the right answers; it requires sharing (and living) those answers loud enough that we get flack for it. Encourage your group members to consider what stands they can take to risk rejection.

Step 1

Throughout this session, you'll need to be aware of and sensitive to non-Christians in your group. Since the session focuses on the rejection that Christians sometimes experience, non-Christians may feel excluded. There are a few places to be extra careful. For example, avoid using "we" in a way that refers specifically to Christians in Step 2. Also, you might want to skip the question **Would you die for your faith in God?** in Step 4.

Step 3

Use one or more of the following suggestions to broaden your kids' understanding of the Bible. Explain that John the Baptist was Jesus' cousin, that he prepared people for the arrival of the Messiah (Jesus), and that many of his disciples later became Jesus' disciples. You might also explain the reference to Isaiah in Matthew 3 and Luke 3. When a king was scheduled to travel through an area, he sent people ahead (forerunners) to repair the road (make it straight, level it, and fill in the potholes). You might also explain that although Matthew and Luke are recording the same events, they emphasize different parts of the story. This is due to the fact that they are addressing different audiences, with different purposes.

Step 1

Instruct group members to close their eyes and imagine what kind of alien they would want to be if they could. Then give distribute paper and pencils and have group members write a description or draw a picture of their "alien selves." After a few minutes, have them read their descriptions or exhibit their pictures. Encourage them to explain why they would want to be that kind of alien. Then have them imagine how people might respond to such a creature.

Step 5

Many of the psalms express the pain of rejection as well as the comfort of God's presence and His faithfulness to His people. Wrap up the session with a worship service based on the psalms. If group members have favorite psalms that are appropriate for the topic, use them. Otherwise, you might use some of the following: Psalm 23, which describes how God protects us from enemies, or Psalms 31, 35, 56, or 57, in which the psalmist talks about being beset by enemies and asks for God's protection. You could have individuals read the psalms (or pertinent portions of them) or do some group readings. You might want to close the service with a gospel song or hymn like "What a Friend We Have in Jesus."

Step 3

As you discuss John the Baptist and his lack of concern about acceptance, ask your group members whether they think girls or guys find it easier not to care about what other people think. Then ask group members to share how much they are affected by what other people think. Ask: **If personal acceptance has a higher priority for you than it should, what can you do about it?**

Step 5

The possibility of rejection can be a very sensitive issue. Discuss the difference between being rejected because of your personality or appearance and being rejected because of your faith and your commitment to God. Ask: **When is it difficult to tell why you're being rejected? What can a person do when he or she feels rejected?**

Step 1

Play a game of "keep away," pitting "aliens" against "earthlings." To determine who are the aliens, choose a physical characteristic such as being left handed, having dark hair, or being shorter than five and a half feet. All those who have that characteristic are aliens. After the teams have played "keep away" (using a ball or any other soft, non-breakable object you have around) for a while, discuss the game. Talk about how the opposing teams treated each other; then compare it to the way people often treat others who are different from them.

Step 5

As you discuss rejection, have your group members concentrate on areas of potential rejection, areas in which following Christ might mean failing to be an "all-American guy." To do this, have your group members come up with a composite description of an "all-American guy." List group members' suggestions on the board as they are given. (Or, if someone in the group has an artistic bent, have him draw a basic figure and add details to reflect the various characteristics.) If your group members need help in coming up with suggestions, prompt them to think about what they're supposed to be like when it comes to drinking (e.g., being able to "hold their liquor"), language, sex, sports, school work, and so on. When they've finished the composite description, discuss how being a Christian might affect a person's ability to be an "all-American guy."

Step 1

Begin the session with a "party-mix" game. Distribute paper and pencils. Instruct group members to each write down the name of a famous person (actor, politician, athlete, etc.). Then have them imagine that they are the people whose names they wrote. They should imagine that they're at a large party in Beverly Hills. As the party progresses, the people gradually group together in different parts of the mansion. (You could designate certain parts of the room as areas of the mansion. One corner could be the pool, another corner could be the ballroom, etc.) Have group members begin mingling. Explain that within five minutes each person should hook up with a group of at least three other people that his or her person would be likely to hang out with. After five minutes, have the members of each group introduce themselves and explain why they're in that group and why they're not in other groups. Discuss how similarities and differences affect the groups we form.

Step 5

Try a more creative and fun way to introduce discussion of the word "blessed." You'll need at least seven "letter cubes" (dice that have letters on them instead of numbers) for this activity. (These letter cubes could be found in a game like "Boggle.") Make sure each cube has one of the letters of the word "blessed" on it and that together the cubes can spell out the entire word. Have each group member take turns rolling the cubes, trying to spell out "blessed." The object of the game is to spell out the entire word using the least number of rolls.

Step 1

Bring in and show some short video clips of aliens from various movies. (Make sure you've screened the clips beforehand.) Have group members try to guess the movies. Here are some possibilities:
- *Star Wars*
- *Close Encounters of the Third Kind*
- *E.T.*
- *The Day the Earth Stood Still*
- *The Thing*
- *V*
- Any of the *Star Trek* movies

Step 2

Before the session, get some volunteers (perhaps members of your group or some adult volunteers) to script and perform a monologue for each of the three Christian character types. You might have the volunteers develop monologues on a similar subject. For example, you could have them all address the topic of junior high kids listening to heavy metal music. Record or videotape these monologues; then play them back for your group members at the beginning of this step.

Step 1

Rather than taking the time to have teams brainstorm descriptions of the aliens, read aloud the following description and have group members respond to it. Explain: **The aliens have three arms and three legs. Each of their hands has ten fingers on it; each of their feet has ten toes on it. They communicate with sounds that resemble human sneezes. They sleep upside down. They greet each other by kissing, using one of the three mouths on their face.** Ask group members how they think people would respond if they met one of these aliens and why.

Step 4

Skip the opening questions of this step. On the "To Die For" sheet, rather than having group members check one of the letters next to each statement, simply have them circle the belief statements that they would be willing to die for. After a minute or two, ask a couple of volunteers to share which statements they circled and why.

Step 3

Use the following questions to help group members determine how people in an urban society today would perceive John the Baptist.
Team 1: What do you think John the Baptist would look like today? What kind of clothes would he wear? Where would he live? What would he smell like? How would he act?
Team 2: How would people in today's urban society react to John the Baptist's message?
Team 3: What kind of people today would reject John the Baptist?
Team 4: What kind of people today would accept John the Baptist's message with no problems?
Team 5: What would happen to John the Baptist in today's society?

Also, when the activity is completed, you might have group members list persons in their own cultural history and/or contemporary experience who have prepared a way for other great leaders.

Step 5

Most urban young people need no introduction to the rejection mentioned in Luke 6:22, 23. Instead, they need to be inspired to help eliminate the rejection others face. Ask: **Do you know people who have been rejected and need someone to share their pain with them?** Have group members write down the names of the people they know who have been rejected because of race, a disability, his or her personality or appearance, etc. Then have them choose one person to encourage or comfort this week. Then, as a group, choose one person for whom you can all do something this week. As you wrap up the session, have someone read aloud Acts 4:32-37.

Step 1

Instead of the alien activity, which some high schoolers might find too childish, have group members think about cliques and the idea of "belonging" at their schools. Have group members form pairs. (Ideally the members of each pair should be from the same school.) Distribute poster board and markers to each pair. Instruct the members of each pair to draw a map or diagram of their school, showing where different groups of kids hang out. Encourage the pairs to consider several different types of groups (jocks, druggies, brains, nerds, socialites, etc.). Give the pairs a few minutes to work. As the pairs explain their drawings, discuss them. Ask: **How do these groups form? How do they view each other? Why don't the members of different groups fit in with each other?** Encourage group members to think about the relationship between differences and acceptance or rejection.

Step 5

To more specifically focus your discussion of rejection, ask your junior highers: **Have you or any of your junior high friends ever been rejected by a high schooler? If so, what happened? How did you or your friend feel? How did you or your friend handle the situation?** Ask your high schoolers: **Have you or any of your high school friends ever rejected a junior higher? If so, what happened? Why did you or your friend do it? How did you or your friend feel about it afterward?**

Step 3

Adapt the Bible study plan so that your sixth graders are focusing on just one short passage in their teams. Have group members form three teams. Assign each team to read Matthew 3:1-12 and answer one of the first three "team" questions. (Assign each team a specific question.) Give the teams a few minutes to work; then have them share their responses. When they're finished, go through questions four and five together as a group.

Step 4

Ask your sixth graders to consider filling in additional items as they work on "To Die For" (Repro Resource 5). After the kids have completed the sheet, give them each two pieces of paper and a pencil. On one piece they should write one "to-die-for" belief. On the other piece they should write a belief that isn't such a high priority. Collect the papers and make a list of the "to-die-for" beliefs and the low-priority beliefs. Refer to these lists as you ask group members to discuss some reasons behind their decisions.

Date Used:

Approx.
Time

Step 1: Invasion   _____
o Small Group
o Little Bible Background
o Fellowship & Worship
o Mostly Guys
o Extra Fun
o Media
o Short Meeting Time
o Combined Junior High/High School
Things needed:

Step 2: Alien Behavior   _____
o Extra Action
o Large Group
o Media
Things needed:

Step 3: Alien Prophet   _____
o Extra Action
o Small Group
o Heard It All Before
o Little Bible Background
o Mostly Girls
o Urban
o Sixth Grade
Things needed:

Step 4: To Die For   _____
o Short Meeting Time
o Sixth Grade
Things needed:

Step 5: Pain of Rejection _____
o Large Group
o Heard It All Before
o Fellowship & Worship
o Mostly Girls
o Mostly Guys
o Extra Fun
o Urban
o Combined Junior High/High School
Things needed:

Blind Faith

YOUR GOALS FOR THIS SESSION:

C h o o s e   o n e   o r   m o r e

☐ To help group members discover what it means to have faith.

☐ To help group members acknowledge that while it's difficult to believe in things they can't see, they still can trust God.

☐ To help group members understand that their faith is in a trustworthy God.

☐ Other _____

Your Bible Base:

Hebrews 11

Mousetrap

(Needed: Two mousetraps, one long pencil, one-dollar bill, a bag or box [optional])

This is an excellent opener, but it takes a little preparation. Go to a hardware store and pick up a couple of mousetraps. Rig one of the traps so that it can't be set off. In other words, hook it in the "loaded" position, so that it cannot be sprung. You can do this by bending the trigger wire and slipping it through the hole in the catch.

Test the trap several times to make sure you've done this right. If you're not absolutely positive about it, don't use this activity. Otherwise you might have to call Jenny's parents and explain, "Well, about your daughter's fingers . . ."

Try to make your adjustment to the one trap as unnoticeable as possible. (Don't have the trigger wire sticking out at a strange angle.) Hide both traps out in the hallway in a big bag or box. Don't let any of your group members know you have the traps.

To start the session, ask for two volunteers to participate in a demonstration of faith. Excuse yourself and step out into the hall. Make sure kids can hear you but not see you. Set the first trap (the non-rigged one). Act as if you're worried about getting hurt (you might!). You could let the trap snap once while setting it so your group members hear the sound.

Bring this trap back into the room, carrying it very carefully so that it won't go off prematurely. (This will create some tension.) Give a long pencil to the first volunteer and ask him or her to show the power of the trap by setting it off. Make sure you are holding the trap by the base to avoid any unplanned pain! Also make sure that the volunteer holds the pencil by the very end, and puts it in the trap without putting his or her fingers in as well. The trap should snap shut quickly and powerfully on the pencil.

Then tell the group that you're going to set the trap for the second volunteer. Take the first trap back into the hall and let it snap shut once so it sounds like you're having a hard time setting it. Then take the second trap (the rigged one) and slip a folded dollar bill onto its bait holder. Bring the second trap out just as carefully as the first—making it seem as though it could go off at any moment.

Tell the second volunteer: **If you can get this dollar, it's yours. Trust me; you won't get hurt.** If the volunteer is too reluctant, encourage the person by reassuring him or her that you can be trusted. If the volunteer still won't take the bait, select a new volunteer.

After the dollar is taken, expose the whole setup to your group members, explaining that they just saw faith in action.

Ask: **How much faith did** (name of the second volunteer) **have to have in me?**

Suppose you knew ahead of time that the trap was rigged. How much faith would you have had? A lot? A little? About the same? If some kids say they would have had a lot of faith, ask them what made them have so much faith.

STEP

2

Seeing Isn't Always Believing

(Needed: One piece of paper)

Stand up if you agree with this statement: Seeing is believing. Ask whoever stands why he or she agrees with this statement.

Is there ever a time when you don't have to see something to believe it?

Wad up a piece of paper and hold it up in the air. Ask: **If I let go of this paper, what will happen to it?** (It will fall to the ground.)

How do you know it will drop or fall? (Gravity will cause it to.)

Stand up if you've seen gravity before. Pay attention to which group members stand.

Now stand if you've never seen gravity. Again, pay attention to which group members stand.

Then explain: **None of us has ever seen gravity! It's an invisible magnetic force. We've all seen the effects of gravity, but no one's ever seen gravity itself.**

Drop the wad of paper. Then tear a small piece from the wad, lay it in the middle of your palm, and lift your hand to your mouth.

Ask: **What would happen to this piece of paper if I blow it?** The group comedian might say something like, "It'll burn up from your breath!" But most kids will probably point out that the paper will fly away.

Explain: **Just as with gravity, none of us have ever seen wind, but we've all seen the effects of wind.** Blow the piece of paper off your hand. **In a way, God is like this. None of us has seen God.**

Ask: **Is it easy or hard for you to have faith in a God you can't see? Why?**

STEP 3

The Sure Thing

(Needed: Slips of paper, copies of Repro Resource 6, pencils, Bibles)

OPTIONS

Distribute slips of paper and pencils to your group members. Explain: **We're going to play a game called "Dictionary." In this game, I choose a word, and you write a definition for that word. Once all the definitions have been collected, we'll read them aloud. Then you'll choose the one you think is the correct definition. The word I want you to define is "faith."**

As kids write down their definitions, you write one too, based on Hebrews 11:1. It might be a good idea to rephrase it in your own words, in case any of your group members have memorized the verse.

When kids have finished, collect the definitions and add yours to the pile. Have kids take turns choosing a definition and reading it aloud. After each one has been read, have group members vote on whether they think that particular definition is the right one. Keep track of the votes. Reread the definition that received the most votes.

If it's the definition from Hebrews 11:1, ask: **How many of you knew that definition was in the Bible? Listen to how God's Word defines or describes faith in Hebrews 11:1: "Now faith is being sure of what we hope for and certain of what we do not see."**

If it's not the statement from Hebrews 11:1, ask: **Why did you pick this definition?**

After a few kids explain their reasoning, say: **Listen to how the Bible describes faith in Hebrews 11:1: "Now faith is being sure of what we hope for and certain of what we do not see." It's a little weird to talk about being sure of things we can't see, but instead of going on and on, the author of Hebrews decided to describe real-life examples of people who were sure of what they hoped for and certain of what they couldn't see.**

Before the session, you'll need to cut apart copies of "Faith Hall of Fame" (Repro Resource 6). Have group members form teams of two or three. Distribute one or more slips to each team.

Explain: **You might recognize some of these Faith Hall of Fame inductees. Some of them are pretty famous. For your inductee, read the assigned passage from Hebrews 11 and his or her "stats." Then decide whether it was easy or hard for this person to have faith, and come up with one reason why this person should be honored in the Faith Hall of Fame.**

Give the teams about ten minutes to work. Then ask each team the following questions as it makes its presentation.

What is the name of your inductee?

Tell us one significant stat about your inductee.

Was it easy or hard for this person to have faith?

Why should your inductee be honored?

Use the following information to supplement the teams' responses.

• Noah should be honored because he trusted God and did the right thing, even when everyone thought he was crazy. Noah was right in the end.

• Abraham should be honored because he trusted God even when God seemed to go against His word. Abraham had confidence in God's promise.

• Moses should be honored because he followed God's plan for His people, instead of having a cushy life in the palace of the pharaoh. He led all those people out of Egypt and parted the Red Sea—with God's help, of course.

• Joshua should be honored because he trusted God's plans for Jericho and destroyed the city.

• Rahab should be honored because she had faith to take the God of Israel at His word. She wanted to be identified with the one true God.

• Gideon should be honored because he trusted God in spite of his weaknesses, and led a small army to a huge victory over the Midianites.

Ask: **What do these inductees have in common?** (They accomplished fantastic things for God. They trusted God even when they didn't know how things would turn out. They obeyed God.)

Say: **These people are like the superstars of the Bible. Everything turned out great for them; so does that mean faith makes everything turn out all right? Why or why not?**

Point out that if you take Hebrews 11 at face value, it does appear that faith guarantees a happy ending—until you read verses 35-40.

Explain: **This might come as bad news for some of you, but trusting God doesn't guarantee that life is going to be great. Look at the list of unnamed people in Hebrews 11:35-40, who are also in the Faith Hall of Fame. What happened to some of them?** (They were tortured, imprisoned, stoned, sawed in two, killed by the sword, went about destitute, persecuted, and mistreated. They wandered in deserts, mountains, and caves.)

Then say: **There comes a point when someone says, "Based on what I know about God, I'm going to trust Him." All of** these **Faith Hall of Fame** inductees got to that point, where they believed God, no matter what. He's the sure thing.

STEP

4

The Real Thing

(Needed: Chalkboard and chalk or newsprint and marker)

Do you think you might end up in the Faith Hall of Fame? Why or why not? Most of your kids probably will say no.

You could get the impression from Hebrews 11 that only the super spiritual are honored for their faith. But did you know that this group includes a murderer (Moses)**, a cheat** (Jacob)**, a prostitute** (Rahab)**, and a coward** (Gideon)**?**

But all of these people got to the point where they believed God, no matter what. That's real faith in the sure thing—God Himself.

Ask two kids who like to perform for a crowd to help you out with two short improvisations.

Explain: **I'm going to give these two a scene to act out. When I say "stop," the rest of you will have a chance to give some advice and explain why they can trust God.**

To the actors, say: **For the first improv, talk about doubts you have about God. You wonder if God cares about you, and worry about bad things happening to you. Ready? Start talking.**

After about a minute, yell "stop." Then get the rest of the group members to call out answers and advice they might have. Use the following suggestions to supplement group members' ideas.

• It's OK to trust God even if you have doubts.

• Even if things are bad, God is in control.

• We should put our trust in God, not in circumstances and appearances.

If your group members get into these improvs, get two different kids to do the second one.

Say: **For the second improv, talk about wanting God to prove Himself in a big way. If God would do something spectacular, then you would have faith in Him. Ready? Start talking.**

Again, go for another minute, then yell "stop." Have group members call out answers and advice. Use the following suggestions to supplement group members' ideas.

• God doesn't need to "prove" Himself. After all, He is God.

• Bible people such as Joshua and Daniel did see some amazing things happen, but even they didn't know what the outcome would be. They obeyed God and trusted His plans.

• Many other people have trusted God even when things have gone from bad to worse.

STEP 5

Picture-Perfect Faith

(Needed: Instant camera, film, construction paper, poster board, glue, markers)

Say: **You don't have to be perfect to have faith, and your faith doesn't have to be perfect. The more you trust God, the more your faith grows. You see, God shows us enough about Himself in the Bible and in Jesus, who came to earth as a man, to let us know that He's in control and that He's trustworthy. We can trust God with the big picture.**

Take out an instant camera and start snapping pictures of your group members. You may want to have group members take pictures of each other too.

Once all the pictures have been developed, explain what you're going to do with them. Say: **We're going to make a collage of our pictures. Mount your picture on a piece of construction paper and write a caption to describe faith in God. When you've finished, we'll glue the pictures on the poster board.**

Encourage kids to be as creative as they want in designing the collage. If they'd like, kids can use a pencil to accent different features of their photos, or draw right on them. When the collage has been put together, ask kids to read and explain the captions. Remember to compliment their creativity.

Close this session in prayer, thanking God for being trustworthy.

Faith Hall of Fame

INDUCTEE: NOAH - Hebrews 11:7
Stats: Noah walked with God even when no one else did. He believed God would send a flood. He followed God's plans completely and built an ark even when everyone laughed at him.

Was it easy or hard for Noah to have faith? _____

Why should Noah be honored in the Faith Hall of Fame?
_____

INDUCTEE: ABRAHAM - Hebrews 11:8-12, 17-19
Stats: Abraham believed God's promise to make him a great nation. He packed his bags and family and headed out to an unknown destination. He trusted God's promise of a son even though it was beyond reason. He obeyed and trusted God even when God told him to give up his one and only son.

Was it easy or hard for Abraham to have faith? _____

Why should Abraham be honored in the Faith Hall of Fame?
_____

INDUCTEE: MOSES - Hebrews 11:23-29
Stats: Moses chose to identify with God's people even though he had it made in Pharaoh's palace. He kept the Passover that God had commanded. He obeyed and trusted God to help him lead over two million people out of slavery in Egypt.

Was it easy or hard for Moses to have faith? _____

Why should Moses be honored in the Faith Hall of Fame?
_____

INDUCTEE: JOSHUA - Hebrews 11:30
Stats: Joshua trusted God even though the strategy to defeat Jericho sounded ridiculous. He obeyed God's command even though it made him and the people look foolish.

Was it easy or hard for Joshua to have faith? _____

Why should Joshua be honored in the Faith Hall of Fame?
_____

INDUCTEE: RAHAB - Hebrews 11:31
Stats: Rahab realized that the one true God was the God of Israel. She risked her life to hide the spies that came into Jericho. She trusted Joshua's God and was rescued while the rest of the city was conquered.

Was it easy or hard for Rahab to have faith? _____

Why should Rahab be honored in the Faith Hall of Fame?
_____

INDUCTEE: GIDEON - Hebrews 11:32-34
Stats: Gideon believed God's purpose for choosing him, even though he thought he was a nobody. He followed God's unusual battle plans and took risks for God because he knew God would be with him.

Was it easy or hard for Gideon to have faith? _____

Why should Gideon be honored in the Faith Hall of Fame?
_____

Step 3

Before the session, cut apart several copies of Repro Resource 6. Distribute the slips to your group members so that each person has several slips with the same character on them. (For instance, one person should have several slips that have "Noah" on them; another person should have several slips that have "Rahab" on them; etc.) The object of the game is for group members to trade slips with each other until they get a slip with each of the six characters on it. The first person to get all six slips is the winner. The catch is that group members won't know how many different slips they have to get. Don't tell them how many different characters they're looking for. Let them keep going until someone thinks he or she has all the slips. However, if a person comes to you with less than six different slips (thinking he or she has them all), he or she is out of the game. To make the game more interesting, you might cut up fewer slips of some characters, making those slips "rarer" and "more valuable" than the others.

Step 5

Have group members form pairs. Instruct each pair to come up with a situation in which someone might need to exercise his or her faith in God or a situation in which that faith might be tested. Then instruct the pairs to think of ways to pantomime their situation to the rest of the group. After a few minutes, have the pairs act out their situations one at a time, while the rest of the group tries to guess the situations. Afterward, discuss how people could strengthen their trust in God in each of the situations.

Step 4

With a small group, you can handle the discussion of doubts in one of several ways. One is to have your group members make a list of the doubts that people might have about trusting God. After group members have suggested several doubts for the list, discuss as a group ways of responding to the doubts. If possible, try to counter each doubt with a biblical truth. (You can use the same method for discussing ways that we often want God to prove Himself to us. [For example: "If I get an 'A' on this test, then I'll know that God really cares about me."]) Another way to address the topic of doubts, especially if you sense that your group members are struggling with them, is to have each group member write a doubt on a slip of paper. Then collect the papers, read them aloud (keeping them anonymous), and let the group respond to them.

Step 5

With a small group, you have the luxury of less-threatening surroundings for personal sharing. Take advantage of this fact as you wrap up the session. Explain to your group members that in the Old Testament, the people who trusted God often had their faith strengthened through experience. Recognizing God's work in their lives probably helped them have stronger faith later. Encourage your group members to strengthen their own and each other's faith by sharing experiences or evidence of God's work in their lives. Remind them that they don't have to have earth-shattering examples (like defeating an army with a few hundred men). You might get them started by sharing an experience or two of your own.

Step 4

Rather than having just two pairs of group members act out a scene, divide the group into teams. Instruct each team to make up a skit or conversation that addresses doubts about God or someone wishing that God would prove Himself in some way. The conversation should include at least one person expressing doubts and at least one person responding with biblical truth. Give the teams a few minutes to work; then have each team act out its conversation. After each team has performed its skit, have the rest of the group offer other suggestions about what to do in the situation. If you think the teams will have difficulty coming up with situations on their own, you may want to do some brainstorming as a group before dividing into teams.

Step 5

You can make this activity more manageable for a large group. Bring in three instant cameras and assign three photographers to take pictures. Have group members form three teams. Assign a photographer and camera to each team. Also distribute construction paper, glue, and markers to each team. Instruct the photographers to take pictures of the members of their teams. When the pictures are developed, have the teams create collages with them. Team 1 should create a collage illustrating how to battle doubt. Team 2 should create a collage illustrating the fact that God is in control of everything. Team 3 should create a collage illustrating faith in God. Give the teams a few minutes to work; then have them share what they came up with.

Step 2

The gravity and wind illustrations may be old hat for kids who've "heard it all before." Instead of covering them one more time, have your group members consider how much faith (of all kinds) plays a part in life. Stimulate their thinking with the following question: **What would happen if you couldn't trust your doctor?** After group members have responded, ask the same question, substituting different people in their lives: cashiers, teachers, cafeteria workers, police officers, pastors, teammates, and so on. You might also point out that the business world depends on trust between people. For example, you couldn't order things by mail if the company didn't trust that you'd pay your bill.

Step 4

Have group members form teams. Instruct each team to write a letter to "a wise person," expressing doubts about God (such as whether or not He really cares) or desires that God would "prove" Himself in some way. Encourage the team members to come up with doubts that are as realistic, persuasive, and tough to answer as possible. When everyone is finished, have each team trade letters with another team. The teams will then read the letters they've received and write a response. When they're finished, have the teams share the letters and responses.

Step 3

To help your group members develop their knowledge of the Bible, provide them with the following Old Testament references for the faith heroes listed on Repro Resource 6.
• Noah—Genesis 6–9
• Abraham—Genesis 12:1–25:18
• Moses—the Books of Exodus, Leviticus, Numbers, and Deuteronomy
• Joshua—Numbers 13:1–14:38; Joshua 1:1–24:33
• Rahab—Joshua 2:1–24; 6:23-25
• Gideon—Judges 6–8

Have group members form teams of three or four. Assign each team one of the characters on Repro Resource 6. Instruct the teams to look up some of the accompanying references to supplement the "stats" of their assigned character on the sheet. With people like Noah, Gideon, and Rahab, the teams could read or skim the entire story; with people like Abraham, Moses, and Joshua, however, the teams should focus on one or two significant events (God's calling of Moses at the burning bush, for example). Encourage the teams to locate these significant events by using the subtitles in their Bibles. (Assist them if necessary.) Encourage the teams to summarize the stories as they present their characters to the group.

Step 4

Kids with little Bible background may have no problem listing doubts about God, but they may have difficulty coming up with advice concerning those doubts. Consequently, they may not be able to improvise conversations. Instead, do this part as a group discussion. Have your group members brainstorm a list of doubts. (Be aware that some kids may be revealing their own doubts.) Discuss these doubts one by one, asking group members to offer advice and supplementing group members' suggestions with your own ideas. (You will probably need to carry the conversation in this activity.)

Step 1

Have group members form pairs. Instruct the members of each pair to come up with a list of as many things as they can think of that they've put their trust in since they woke up this morning. Encourage them to be as wacky, creative, and extreme as possible in their ideas. If they have trouble getting started, use some of the following suggestions.
• **When you brushed your teeth this morning, you put your trust in the fact that the toothpaste manufacturer didn't accidentally put drain cleaner in the toothpaste tube.**
• **When you got in the car to come to the meeting, you put your trust in the fact that no one had tampered with the car's brakes.**
• **When you walked outside, you put your trust in the fact that gravity wouldn't suddenly stop, sending you hurtling into space.**

The pair that comes up with the most ideas wins. Afterward, have the partners discuss why they trust some things without even thinking about them, but have difficulty trusting other things.

Step 5

As you wrap up the session, point out that God has given us other Christians to help and encourage us in our faith. To remind group members of their responsibility to each other, create a collage of your own. While group members are working on their own collages, take a picture of each person. Then cut and arrange the pictures so that group members look like they're posing for a group photo. (For fun, you might want to have your group members try to arrange themselves so that they look like the "group photo" in the collage.) Keep the collage displayed in your meeting area as a reminder of the help other Christians can offer when we struggle with our faith. Then close the session with prayer, praising God for giving us other Christians to help and encourage us.

MOSTLY GIRLS

Step 4

It's usually easier to *talk* about faith in a group than it is to *practice* it when you're alone. Therefore, spend some time talking with your group members about "alone times." Ask: **If you are alone and worried about a major problem, which of the suggestions from these roleplays might help you? Why?** Encourage group members to write down and take home any pertinent ideas.

Step 5

Your group members may prefer to write captions for another person's picture rather than for their own. Therefore, after you've given group members the pictures you took of them, have them trade pictures with one or two other people in the group. In writing captions for the pictures, suggest that group members use statements such as "Sally showed faith in God when she . . ."

MOSTLY GUYS

Step 1

Introduce the idea of trust with the following game. Before the session, prepare a stack of cards. Each card in the stack should say either "own color" or "other color." You'll also need a supply of white balloons, blue balloons, and toothpicks. To begin, clear an area in the room. Divide the balloons among group members so that there is an equal number of blue balloons and white balloons. Have each group member blow up his balloon and fasten it behind him by taping or tying it to his belt or belt loop. Then have each group member draw a card (keeping its message secret) and take a toothpick. The object is for group members to pop balloons of the color indicated by their cards. However, as group members are popping others' balloons, they must keep from getting their own balloons popped. The difficulty is that they don't know who to trust. The last person with an unpopped balloon wins. Afterward, discuss the difficulties of the game, especially of not knowing who to trust.

Step 3

Instead of having them play "Dictionary," get your group members thinking about how faith relates to being a man. Point out that our society often emphasizes self-sufficiency, especially for guys. Men aren't supposed to need other people for help or support. Instead, they are supposed to be able to solve their own problems. Get group members thinking about these expectations by having them answer "does" or "doesn't" to the following questions: **(1) A real man does/doesn't ask for directions. (2) A real man does/doesn't depend on others to help him. (3) A real man does/doesn't admit that a problem could be bigger than he can handle.** Continue discussing other pressures on males to be self-reliant. Then explain that many men in the Bible were heroes of faith because they knew that real men trust God.

EXTRA FUN

Step 1

In your meeting area, create a maze or obstacle course of chairs. Have group members form pairs for a race. Explain that one member of each pair will be directing his or her partner (who will be blindfolded) through the maze. However, the person doing the guiding will not be able to talk to or touch his or her partner. Give the members of each pair a minute or two to come up with a series of nonverbal signals to indicate directions. (For instance, two hand claps might indicate "take two steps forward"; one foot stomp might indicate "turn right.")Then blindfold one person in each pair. When you say, **Go**, his or her partner will begin directing him or her through the obstacle course. (If possible, you might want to bring a stopwatch to time the pairs' efforts. You might even want to award prizes to the pair that completes the course in the shortest amount of time.) Afterward, discuss the importance of being able to trust your partner's guidance.

Step 5

End the session on a fun note with another blindfold game. Have your group members form a loose circle with two people in the middle. The two in the middle should be blindfolded. Each should have a rattle. One of them will be the pursuer; the other will be the pursued. The object of the game for the pursuer is to "capture" (tag) the pursued. The object of the game for the pursued is to elude the pursuer. The rules of the game are simple. When one shakes his or her rattle, the other must rattle back immediately. (The players will use the rattle sounds to determine the location of each other.) The pursuer may only initiate the rattling five times. If he or she has not tagged the pursuer ten seconds after the fifth rattle, he or she loses. Let the group members on the sideline keep track of the number of rattles, make distracting comments, and move around to change the boundaries. Continue switching pairs until everyone has had a chance to play.

Step 3
Have group members form teams of two or three. Assign one of the characters from "Faith Hall of Fame" (Repro Resource 6) to each team. Explain that you're going to make an audiotape or videotape for the Faith Hall of Fame display. Instruct the teams to think about what their character would say to junior high kids about faith. Have them write a 30-60 second statement, choose a team member to read it, and then record or videotape the statement. When everyone is finished, play the teams' tapes and discuss them as a group.

Step 5
Instead of making a collage of instant-camera prints, bring a video camera and make a group faith video. Have each group member make up a personal description of faith, about 15-30 seconds long. Then record group members giving their descriptions. Not only can you use the tape in this session, you can play it for your group periodically over the next few months and years to see if group members' opinions have changed.

Step 1
If you're short on time, you can skip this step or try a simpler and quicker alternative. Ask for three volunteers. Instruct one of them to fall backward, keeping his or her eyes closed and remaining stiff as a board. Instruct the other two to catch the person. Afterward, discuss how trusting the first volunteer was. Did he or she flinch, bend, or try to catch himself or herself at the last minute? Then discuss what kinds of things determine how much faith you have in the people catching you (e.g., how strong they are, how dependable they are, etc.).

Step 5
If you don't have time to take pictures of your group members and make a group collage, try creating a group "autograph sheet" instead. You'll need a large sheet of poster board and several different-colored markers. Instruct each group member to write on the poster board his or her personal definition or description of faith and then sign his or her name. Afterward, go through the definitions and descriptions, asking group members to comment on or clarify what they wrote.

Step 3
After discussing the "Faith Hall of Fame," inform your group members that they will be involved in the "First Annual Faith Academy Awards" in your church or community. Explain that your youth group will be awarding certificates to people who have exemplified godly faith and have modeled the Christian life for all urban teens. Give your group members a few minutes to brainstorm a list of people in the church or community to nominate for the awards. Point out that the process of election ought to use the same fourfold criteria your group members used in choosing "Faith Hall of Fame" inductees. Discuss the list of names your group members come up with. Then narrow your choices down to the specified number of awards you want to present. You might want to consider making these award presentations publicly by inviting the recipients to your next youth group meeting (or church service). You might even consider listing the recipients' names in the local community newspaper.

Step 4
With an urban group, you might want to consider using the following two improvisational situations.
• **For the first improv, talk about how faith in God's power and individual action can help a "crack head"** (drug addict) **get away from drugs and into treatment to get his or her life in order.**
• **For the second improv, talk about why some Christians are very poor and others are very rich.** In their discussion, instruct the volunteers to address this question: "Is it because the rich Christians pray more and the poor ones have a lack of faith, or is there another reason?"

Step 2

The illustrations of gravity and the wind may seem easy (or overly familiar) to your high school students. So instead of using these illustrations, get group members thinking about the relationship between belief and sight by staging a debate on this proposition: "Seeing is believing." Have group members form two teams. One team will argue that the proposition is true; the other will argue that it's false. Give the teams a few minutes to come up with some arguments to support their positions. Then allow each team an opportunity to present its view. (A minute or two should suffice.) Give each team an opportunity to respond to its opponent. After some debate, help your group members see how this issue relates to belief in God. Point out that although we can't see God, we can see evidence of His existence and results of His activity.

Step 5

Read the following list of situations in which a person might have difficulty trusting God. After you read each one, have group members call out whether the situation would probably affect a high schooler or a junior higher more, and why. Afterward, have your group members offer suggestions on how a person might increase his or her trust in God in each situation. If possible, have your junior highers offer suggestions for the high school situations and your high schoolers offer suggestions for the junior high situations. The situations are as follows:
- **Getting into a good college**
- **Going to school the day after you get a bad haircut**
- **Finding a summer job**
- **Finding a boyfriend or girlfriend**
- **Taking a test you're nervous about**
- **Telling your parents you flunked a class**
- **Not making a sports team/ cheerleading squad**

Step 3

Before your sixth graders work on "Faith Hall of Fame" (Repro Resource 6), have them form six teams. Give each team the name of one of the Faith Hall of Fame inductees. Instruct each team to tell the story of its inductee to the rest of the group. In its story, however, each team should include one piece of misinformation. After each story is told, have the rest of the group members try to identify what is true and what is not true about the inductee's experiences.

Step 5

As your sixth graders are writing captions for their pictures, talk about the things we do to show our faith in God. Ask: **In what way is reading the Bible and praying demonstrating faith? What about things like showing respect for teachers and parents?**

Date Used:

Approx.
Time

Step 1: Mousetrap _____
o Fellowship & Worship
o Mostly Guys
o Extra Fun
o Short Meeting Time
Things needed:

Step 2: Seeing Isn't Always Believing _____
o Heard It All Before
o Combined Junior High/High School
Things needed:

Step 3: The Sure Thing _____
o Extra Action
o Little Bible Background
o Mostly Guys
o Media
o Urban
o Sixth Grade
Things needed:

Step 4: The Real Thing _____
o Small Group
o Large Group
o Heard It All Before
o Little Bible Background
o Mostly Girls
o Urban
Things needed:

Step 5: Picture-Perfect Faith _____
o Extra Action
o Small Group
o Large Group
o Fellowship & Worship
o Mostly Girls
o Extra Fun
o Media
o Short Meeting Time
o Combined Junior High/High School
o Sixth Grade
Things needed:

The Price Jesus Paid

YOUR GOALS FOR THIS SESSION:

Choose one or more

☐ To help group members realize the price Jesus paid for their sins.

☐ To help group members understand God's plan of salvation.

☐ To help group members respond to Christ by choosing to follow Him.

☐ Other _____
_____

Your Bible Base:

John 18—19
Galatians 2:20

STEP
I

The Punishment Fits the Crime

(Needed: Two chairs, table, an adult volunteer, extra props [optional])

O P T I O N S

EXTRA ACTION

SMALL GROUP

FELLOWSHIP & WORSHIP

EXTRA FUN

MEDIA

SHORT MEETING TIME

JR.HIGH HIGH SCHOOL COMBINED

Open the session with a courtroom simulation designed to help group members understand what we mean when we say "Christ paid the penalty for our sin."

You can act out this simulation simply with two chairs and a table. But the more you can make your meeting place look like a courtroom, the better it will be. Some ideas for props include elevating the judge's desk and chair, giving the judge a gavel (or hammer) and a robe to wear, roping off a seating area as a jury box, and using a podium for a witness stand.

In addition to the props, you need to recruit someone to play the part of the judge. Ideally, this person should be another adult, but not one of your other leaders. You also could ask a high school student that your junior highers don't know very well. This person should have a little acting ability and a knack for improvising. Also, the simulation calls for the judge to be slapped, so your willing victim should agree to go along with this. *Don't* use one of your own junior highers.

You and your recruit should run through the simulation together, to get an idea of what will happen and what to say. You'll play the part of the bailiff.

One final preparation step is to think of a junior higher—someone who will be at the meeting—who can be the accused. Don't tell this person what you're up to; but make sure you choose someone who feels comfortable in front of the group and who can take a joke. It might be a good idea to choose a boy, because your group members might feel a bit more sympathetic toward a girl—and you *want* the group to reach a verdict of guilty.

As group members arrive for this session, direct them to sit in the "jury area." Explain to them that they will be the jury in a very serious criminal case.

Then announce: **All rise, this court is now in session. The honorable Judge _____ presiding.** The judge enters and takes his or her lofty seat. Then the group may be seated again.

You, the bailiff, read the charges: **The charges against the defendant are as follows: failure to clean his room, disobeying his parents, not paying attention in school, spending too much money on junk, and resisting arrest. The name of the**

charged is _____.

Bring the accused to the witness stand. The judge will then list the charges again, giving more detail for each one. Here is where your judge can have some fun. He or she should embellish the charges, making them sound as if they were the most horrible crimes a person could commit. The judge should provide evidence, false as it may be, to prove that these charges are true.

When all the charges have been read, the judge instructs the jury (the rest of the group members) on the severity of the charges and urges them to make a decision that is fair and just.

As mentioned previously, you want the jury to reach a guilty verdict. Most junior highers will come to this conclusion very rapidly. If you think you might have a sympathetic jury on your hands, inform a couple of key kids beforehand to sway the group to a guilty verdict. After the verdict is reached, the jury reports to the judge who, in true courtroom manner, beats the gavel and pronounces the defendant guilty.

The judge should pause, look over some notes, and then give his or her decision on the penalty: **A verdict of guilty has been reached. The penalty for these crimes is a hard slap across the face. The sentence will be served now.**

As the bailiff, you should walk over to the defendant, ask him to stand, and in full view of the audience, wind up as if to slap him across the face. Just before you swing (the defendant probably will be ducking anyway), the judge should yell out: **Wait! It's true that this guy is guilty. It's also true that the punishment must be carried out. But because I care for him, I will take his punishment for him.**

The judge should descend from his or her chair, take off his or her robe, and solemnly walk over to you. In full view of the group, slap him or her across the face. The slap needs to be hard enough to surprise the group members, yet not hard enough to hurt the judge beyond a little stinging. Be sure to take off any rings, and be very careful to avoid the person's ears.

While it's tempting to alter this part of the simulation with a funny punishment, it is important that the punishment be something *none* of the kids in the group want. If the punishment is doing some crazy stunt, there would undoubtedly be some in the group who would wish they were up front getting the attention. Again, if the judge is played by a leader or a friend or peer of your group members, then some of the impact may be taken away—your group members might think it's funny.

Once the punishment has been administered, the judge should walk out of the room without saying a word. Quickly step forward and start discussing the simulation immediately.

Ask: **What are you thinking right now?**
Did the defendant deserve to get slapped? Why?
Did the judge deserve to get slapped? Why or why not?

Why do you think the judge took the defendant's punishment for him?

Did anything bother you about the judge taking the punishment instead of the guilty person? (It didn't seem fair for the innocent person to be punished while the guilty person got off. Guilty people should pay some kind of price—that's how life works.)

Did this scene remind you of anything? Some of your kids may mention Jesus taking the punishment for our sin, which would be absolutely right.

Whipping Boy

There's a story about a prince who had a "whipping boy." **Whenever the bratty prince did something wrong, his whipping boy would get whipped.**

Suppose you had a grounding boy who got grounded each time you did something wrong. What do you think of the concept? It probably sounds like a great concept to your kids.

How do you think a person would end up as a whipping boy? (The person probably was forced into it, because he didn't have any rights or say in the matter. Or maybe the whipping boy was paying back some wrong *he* had done.)

In a way, Jesus was like the world's whipping boy, but there's a major difference. He *chose* to take the punishment for our sins because we were totally helpless to do anything about it ourselves.

STEP 3

No Pain, No Gain

(Needed: Bibles, copies of Repro Resource 7, pencils)

Have your group members turn to John 18 and 19. Say: **I know some of you have heard or read the story of Jesus' death before; but whether it's the hundredth time or the first time you've heard the story, pay attention to the details.**

Read aloud John 18:1-5, 12, 13, 19-24, 28-40; 19:1-19, 28-30. It might be a good idea to put some lightly penciled check marks in your Bible ahead of time next to the verses you'll be reading, so you won't have to stop every few verses to check the references.

When you've finished reading, pass out copies of "Did You Know?" (Repro Resource 7) and pencils. Work through the sheet with your group, reading each statement and letting group members check the boxes. (Some of the items have been taken from the other Gospel accounts.) This should be a rather serious time as you help your group members focus on what Jesus did for them. Feel free to stop at any point and discuss questions they may have.

Then say: **Whoa! This is heavy stuff to think about. How do you feel about what Jesus suffered for us?**

Why do you think Jesus went through all this? Did He want to do this? Did He deserve to die? As kids talk about these questions, reassure them that Jesus wasn't a masochist (someone who enjoys pain), but His suffering had a purpose—to take away the sins of the world.

Say: **Jesus' pain was our gain. What were some of the things we gained? When you think of a gain, tell it to the person next to you; then the two of you should stand up and say the gain together.**

If you'd like, mention some of the following gains to different kids to get things started:

• Our sins are forgiven.
• We can have a right relationship with God.
• We can have eternal life.
• We become children of God.

Explain: **One thing we have to understand is that we're not forced to accept Jesus' payment for our sin. We have to make that choice ourselves.**

OPTIONS

LARGE GROUP

HEARD IT ALL BEFORE

LITTLE BIBLE BACKGROUND

MOSTLY GIRLS

SHORT MEETING TIME

URBAN

SIXTH GRADE

STEP
4

The Choice

(Needed: Bibles, index cards, pencils)

You probably know your group members well enough to know who has and hasn't made a decision to accept the free gift of salvation offered to us by Jesus' death on the cross. If you think there are some kids who don't know the Lord, take some time to explain how they can become part of God's family. Here are some steps to help you.

• God wants everyone to enjoy the best life possible and experience His love (Jeremiah 31:3).

• But everyone has blown it in a big way—this is called sin and rebellion against God (Romans 3:23).

• This would separate us from God forever—and we, the guilty ones, deserve to pay the penalty (Romans 6:23).

• Only God could solve the problem, and He did. He sent His Son, Jesus, to die (John 3:16, 17; Romans 5:8).

• But we're not forced to accept God's solution. We need to repent of our sins and personally commit ourselves to Him (Acts 20:21).

• We can have forgiveness. If a person receives Jesus as who He claimed to be and believes that God raised Jesus from the dead, God has promised that person eternal life (John 1:12; Romans 10:9; 1 John 5:11).

Distribute index cards. Have each person turn to Galatians 2:20 and write the verse on one side of the card. After your group members have finished copying the verse, discuss what it means. Then challenge kids to write a personal statement to God about following Him. Tell them you won't be collecting their responses; this is a matter between them and God.

Say: **Under the verse you just copied down, sign your name if you want the verse to be a true statement for you. Or just sign "Paul"—the writer of the verse—if you're not ready to make this kind of a commitment.**

By having all group members write something, no one should feel pressured to answer in a certain way. Have group members put their cards in their Bibles or pockets. *Don't* collect the cards.

Close your time in prayer, thanking Jesus for paying the price for our sin and making salvation possible.

Many junior highers think they need to accept God's forgiveness over and over again. You might want to have one or two adults ready to talk

privately with anyone who wants to become a Christian or who has
doubts about his or her commitment to Christ.

Did You Know?

Check one of the boxes after each statement.

	I knew that.	I didn't know that.
1. Jesus was turned in by one of His close friends and disciples.		
2. All of Jesus' disciples deserted Him the night He was arrested.		
3. The guards blindfolded Jesus and punched Him.		
4. Jesus never said or did anything to defend Himself while the guards were beating Him.		
5. The guards made fun of Jesus and spit on Him.		
6. The religious leaders had Jesus beaten in their presence. One official hit Jesus in the face.		
7. Jesus was handed from one politician to another because they didn't want to deal with Him.		
8. His own people wanted Jesus killed and an accused murderer released from jail, rather than the other way around.		
9. Jesus was whipped (flogged). The whip probably had nine leather strands with bits of metal or bone embedded in the ends. The whip was flung onto the person's back—so that all the sharp objects stuck—and then pulled down to tear the skin and muscles off the back.		
10. A robe was stuck on Jesus' raw back to mock Him as a king.		

Check one of the boxes after each statement.

	I knew that.	I didn't know that.
11. The "crown of thorns" was most likely made of stiff, two- or three-inch thorns that stuck right into Jesus' head.		
12. Jesus was forced to carry His own cross. Crossbeams alone weighed forty pounds. The cross was made of very rough wood, and rested on Jesus' torn back as He carried it.		
13. Jesus had a big spike pounded through each wrist and one through both feet.		
14. The cross was lifted by soldiers and dropped into a hole in the ground, tearing Jesus' flesh around the spikes.		
15. Death on a cross occurs by suffocation—the victim can't breathe.		
16. Jesus had to hang His weight on the spikes in His wrists until He needed a breath. Then He'd push up on the spike in His feet, scraping His back against the wood, just to take a breath.		
17. The whole time Jesus hung on the cross people made fun of Him.		
18. Jesus may have been naked on the cross.		
19. Jesus could have said at any moment, "OK, that's enough." He could have chosen to stop what was happening to Him.		
20. The soldiers pierced Jesus' side with a spear after He was dead.